Study Guide

for use with

Human Development

Eleventh Edition

Diane E. Papalia
Sally Wendkos Olds
Ruth Duskin Feldman

Prepared by
Peggy Skinner
South Plains College

Boston   Burr Ridge, IL   Dubuque, IA   Madison, WI   New York   San Francisco   St. Louis
Bangkok   Bogotá   Caracas   Kuala Lumpur   Lisbon   London   Madrid   Mexico City
Milan   Montreal   New Delhi   Santiago   Seoul   Singapore   Sydney   Taipei   Toronto

The *McGraw·Hill* Companies

McGraw-Hill Higher Education

Study Guide for use with
HUMAN DEVELOPMENT
Diane E. Papalia, Sally Wendkos Olds, Ruch Duskin Feldman

Published by McGraw-Hill, an imprint of The McGraw-Hill Companies, Inc., 1221 Avenue of the Americas,
New York, NY 10020. Copyright © 2009, 2007, 2004, 2001 by The McGraw-Hill Companies, Inc. All rights
reserved.

1 2 3 4 5 6 7 8 9 0 QPD/QPD 0 9 8

ISBN: 978-0-07-723493-5
MHID: 0-07-723493-6

Table of Contents

PART 1: ABOUT HUMAN DEVELOPMENT

Part I contains Chapters 1 and 2 and is designed to provide you with a guide map to the study of human development. The first chapter discusses the routes that investigators have followed in their quest for information about how people grow and develop, why they proceed to develop in certain ways, and what makes it all possible. The main investigative directions of today and the central questions being posed about human development are also presented.

CHAPTER 1: THE STUDY OF HUMAN DEVELOPMENT

Chapter 1 describes how the study of human development has evolved and introduces the basic goals and concepts of the field. The many influences that make each person a unique individual are introduced and discussed in this chapter.

Guideposts for Study

1. What is human development, and how has its study evolved?
2. What do developmental scientists study?
3. What kinds of influences make one person different from another?
4. What are seven principles of the life-span developmental approach?

Detailed Chapter Outline with Key Terms

I. HUMAN DEVELOPMENT: AN EVER-EVOLVING FIELD
   Human development: Scientific study of these patterns of change and stability. Development is both systematic and adaptive.

   A. Studying the Life Span
      - **Life-span development**: Concept of development as a lifelong process, which can be studied scientifically.
      - Life span studies included Lewis Terman's work with gifted individuals. Paul Baltes has a comprehensive framework for life-span development.

   B. Human Development Today
      1. Goals of a scientific discipline
         - *Description:* Goal in the study of human development in which scientists observe behavior in order to detect patterns or norms in the lives of children and adults.
         - *Explanation:* Goal in which scientists attempt to understand and tell why observed behavior occurs.
         - *Prediction:* Goal in which scientists make educated guesses about what might happen in the future to behavior.
         - *Intervention:* Goal in which scientists use the knowledge of causes of behavior to change or control behavior.

2. Interdisciplinary approach—human development takes information and research from several fields including
- Psychology
- Psychiatry
- Sociology
- Anthropology
- Biology
- Genetics
- Family science
- Education
- History
- Medicine

II. THE STUDY OF HUMAN DEVELOPMENT: BASIC CONCEPTS
A. Domains of Development
- *Domain:* An aspect of the self including physical, cognitive, or psychosocial development.
- **Physical development**: Growth of body and brain, sensory capacities, motor skills, and health.
- **Cognitive development**: Learning, memory, language, thinking, reasoning, and creativity.
- **Psychosocial development**: Emotions, personality, and social relationships.
B. Periods of the Life Span
- **Social construction**: Concept about the nature of reality, based on societally shared perceptions or assumptions.
- Periods include prenatal period, infancy and toddlerhood, early childhood, middle childhood, adolescence, young adulthood, middle adulthood, and late adulthood.

III. INFLUENCES ON DEVELOPMENT
Individual differences: Differences in characteristics, influences, or developmental outcomes.
A. Heredity, Environment, and Maturation
- **Heredity**: Inborn characteristics inherited from biological parent and called "nature."
- **Environment**: Totality of nonhereditary, or experiential, influences on development and called "nurture."
- **Maturation**: Unfolding of a natural sequence of physical and behavioral changes, including readiness to master new abilities.
B. Contexts of Development
  1. Family
  - **Nuclear family**: Kinship and household unit made up of one or two parents and their biological, adopted, and/or stepchildren.
  - **Extended family**: Multigenerational network of grandparents, aunts, uncles, and other relatives, sometimes living together in an *extended-family household*.

2. Socioeconomic Status and Neighborhood
   - **Socioeconomic status (SES)**: Combination of economic and social factors describing an individual or family, including income, education, and occupation.
   - **Risk factors**: Conditions that increase the likelihood of a negative developmental outcome.
3. Culture and Ethnicity
   - **Culture**: A society's or group's total way of life, including customs, traditions, beliefs, laws, knowledge, values, language, and physical products—all learned and shared behavior passed on from parents to children.
   - **Ethnic group**: Group united by distinctive culture, ancestry, religion, language, and/or national origin, all of which contribute to a sense of shared identity and shared attitudes, beliefs, and values.
   - **Ethnic gloss**: overgeneralization about a group.
   - **Acculturate**: adaptation by an immigrant or minority group to get along with the dominant group.
C. Normative and Nonnormative Influences
   - **Normative**: Characteristic of an event that occurs in a similar way for most people in a group.
   - *Normative age-graded influences:* Event or influence that is highly similar for people in a particular age group. Includes biological (puberty, menopause) and social (marriage, retirement) events.
   - *Normative history-graded influences:* Significant environmental events that shape the behavior and attitudes of a particular cohort.
   - **Historical generation:** A group of people who experience an event, such as the Great Depression or 9/11, at a formative time of life.
   - **Cohort**: Group of people born about the same time.
   - **Nonnormative** influences: Unusual events that have a major impact on individual lives because they disturb the expected sequence of the life cycle.
D. Timing of Influences: Critical or Sensitive Periods
   - **Imprinting**: Phenomenon in which newly hatched birds will instinctively follow the first moving object they see, the result of the readiness of the nervous system of the organism to acquire certain information during a brief critical period in early life.
   - **Critical period**: Specific time when a given event, or its absence, has a specific impact on development.
   - **Plasticity**: flexibility or modification of performance.
   - **Sensitive periods**: Times in development when a person is especially responsive to certain kinds of experiences.

IV. BALTES'S LIFE-SPAN DEVELOPMENTAL APPROACH
   1. Development is lifelong.
   2. Development is multidimensional.
   3. Development is multidirectional.
   4. Relative influences of biology and culture shift over the life span.
   5. Development involves changing resource allocations.
   6. Development shows plasticity.

7. Development is influenced by the historical and cultural context.

True/False Self-Test

Place a T or an F in the appropriate space. These questions are taken from the chapter content, tables, key terms, Guideposts for Study, and Checkpoints.

1. ____ Human development focuses primarily upon the first 5 years of life because this is the time for most change.

2. ____ The goals of the developmental research include description, explanation, prediction, and intervention of behavior.

3. ____ Human development uses information from medicine, sociology, and anthropology to explain behavior.

4. ____ The Chippewa Indians have only two periods of childhood, whereas other cultures have more.

5. ____ The view that humans have eight periods of the life span is a social construction.

6. ____ All societies recognize differences in the ways people of different ages think, feel, and act.

7. ____ Most people have dementia and require nursing home care in late adulthood.

8. ____ Socioeconomic status limits people's choices of where to live.

9. ____ Most immigrants have some acculturation to the new society.

10. ____ Biological events such as puberty and menopause are nonnormative events.

11. ____ Loss of a spouse early in a person's 30s is a nonnormative event.

12. ____ The concept of critical periods is more controversial when applied to cognitive and psychosocial development than to physical development.

13. ____ The study of attachment and the development of friendship is an example of cognitive development.

14. ____ Many abilities, such as memory, strength, and endurance, can be significantly improved with training and practice, even late in life.

15. ____ Broad dimensions of personality, such as conscientiousness and openness to new experience, are fixed in early childhood.

16. ____Historically, the nuclear family was the dominant form of family structure in the United States and other Western industrial societies.

17. ____Maturation varies in persons, but averages provide ways to measure what are typical times for development to occur.

18. ____Poor children are at lower risk than wealthy children to have emotional or behavioral problems.

19. ____Children from higher SES families have lower rates of substance abuse, anxiety, and depression than children from lower SES families.

Multiple-Choice Self-Test

Circle the letter of the best answer. These questions are based on many aspects of the chapter content, in no particular order.

1. Dr. Nunez wants to know what child might be at risk for problem behaviors so he can put the child in a special program. He is demonstrating the goal of:
a. description.
b. explanation.
c. prediction.
d. intervention.

2. Dr. George studies how much children grow when they sleep. This is an example of the _____ domain.
a. psychosocial
b. Cognitive
c. physical
d. All of these.

3. Life-span studies in the United States grew out of studies:
a. of primates.
b. of changes in family rules.
c. designed to follow children through adulthood.
d. Of the elderly.

4. Ideas about the nature of reality based on shared subjective perceptions or assumptions are known as:
a. myths.
b. religions.
c. social constructions.
d. realism.

5. A person in young adulthood would be likely to have the developmental task of:
a. getting to know who they are.
b. finding a partner and starting a family.
c. learning another language.
d. preparing for retirement.

6. Paul Baltes is best known for:
a. penicillin.
b. the IQ test.
c. the life-span developmental approach.
d. the Oakland Growth Study.

7. One important characteristic of development is *plasticity*, which refers to:
a. rigidity of ideas.
b. lack of change.
c. modifiability of performance.
d. growing in one direction at a time.

8. Damage in children due to prenatal alcohol exposure is an example of:
a. sensitive periods.
b. critical periods.
c. normative events.
d. history-graded events.

9. Research on memory and learning in older persons is looking at the _____ domain.
a. cognitive
b. physical
c. psychosocial
d. personality

10. Study of inborn traits is looking at:
a. heredity.
b. environment.
c. nurture.
d. maturation.

11. The study of temperament falls in the _____ domain.
a. anxiety.
b. psychosocial development.
c. physical development.
d. cognitive development.

12. The Western world generally divides the life span into _____ periods.
a. two
b. eight
c. four
d. twelve

13. Attachment typically occurs in the period of:
a. adolescence.
b. early childhood.
c. late adulthood.
d. conception to birth.

14. The search for identity typically occurs in:
a. middle adulthood.
b. adolescence.
c. infancy.
d. early childhood.

15. In young adulthood, your health typically:
a. declines.
b. peaks.
c. peaks and declines.
d. remains unchanged.

16. In middle adulthood, a person is most likely to:
a. launch adult children.
b. Care for elderly parents.
c. find new challenges.
d. All of these happen.

17. In late adulthood, most people are:
a. retired or planning to retire.
b. in nursing homes.
c. depressed and lonely.
d. divorced.

18. The search for meaning in life assumes central importance in:
a. late adulthood.
b. middle age.
c. adolescence.
d. young adulthood.

19. Jessica is 10, in school, and lives at home. This is an example of _____ development.
a. nonnormative
b. cohort
c. ethnic gloss
d. normative

20. The unfolding of a natural, genetically influenced sequence of physical changes and behavior patterns is
a. growth.
b. maturation.
c. risk taking.
d. independence.

21. A two-generational household unit consisting of parents and children is:
a. a nuclear family.
b. a tribe.
c. an extended family.
d. a society.

22. The kinds of homes and neighborhoods people live in, as well as the quality of medical care, and other opportunities available to them are examples of:
a. socioeconomic status (SES).
b. stratification.
c. factors associated with socioeconomic status.
d. welfare states.

23. The story of Genie is an example of:
a. plasticity.
b. nurture.
c. critical periods.
d. SES and development.

24. Which of the following statements is FALSE concerning culture?
a. Culture is unchanging.
b. Culture includes tradition.
c. Culture is all of the learned behavior passed on from parents to children.
d. Culture includes art work and tools.

25. Which of the following characteristics of development is NOT one of the characteristics of life-span development, according to Baltes?
a. lifelong
b. multidimensional
c. nonmodifiable
d. multidirectional

Short Essay

These short essay questions are based in part on the Checkpoints in the chapter. Answer each question as completely and succinctly as possible. Check your answers by reviewing the part of the chapter that covers the Guidepost listed with each question.

1. Explain the three domains of development and how they are linked. (See Guidepost 2.)

2. Summarize the central assumptions of Baltes' life-span developmental approach. (See Guidepost 4.)

3. Name four goals of the scientific study of human development. (See Guidepost 2.)

4. Explain why the concept of "critical " periods may more accurately apply to physical than to cognitive development. (See Guidepost 3.)

5. In view of poverty's long-term effects on children's development, what can and should be done to combat it? (See Guidepost 3.)

Organize It!

Making lists is a fun and useful way to organize information in your mind. After making each list, think of ways to memorize it so that you have immediate recall. Singing a list, dancing while you recite it, or simply saying it in a rhythmic pattern as you are walking, driving, or jogging allows your brain to store the information in easily retrievable form. Try it!

1. List the eight periods of the life span, according to the chapter information. (See Table 1-1 and Guidepost 2.)

    1.

    2.

    3.

    4.

    5.

    6.

    7.

    8.

2. List the seven principles of the life-span developmental approach according to Baltes. (See Guidepost 4.)

    1.

    2.

    3.

    4.

    5.

    6.

3. List and briefly describe the four goals of the field of human development (See Guidepost 2.)

    1.

    2.

    3.

    4.

4. List and describe the two major types of families. (See Guidepost 3.)

    1.

    2.

5. List and briefly describe the other disciplines that contribute to human development. (See Guidepost 3.)

    1.

    2.

    3.

    4.

    5.

    6.

Critical Thinking Questions

These questions can be used in small group discussions or, if your instructor agrees, as extra-credit assignments.

1. Do you think there should be more stages in the life span, and, if so, how many? How would you describe the extra stages?

2. How might you be different if you had grown up in a culture other than your own?

3. Can you think of a major cultural event within your lifetime that shaped the lives of families and children? How would you go about studying its effects?

Answer Keys

True/False Self-Test

1. F	GP 2		11. T	GP 2
2. T	GP 2		12. T	GP 2
3. T	GP 3		13. F	GP 2
4. T	GP 1		14. T	GP 3
5. T	GP 1		15. F	GP 3
6. T	GP 2		16. T	GP 3
7. F	GP 2		17. T	GP 3
8. T	GP 3		18. F	GP 3
9. T	GP 3		19. F	GP3
10.F	GP 2			

Multiple-Choice Self-Test

1. d	GP 2		14. b	GP 2
2. c	GP 2		15. b	GP 2
3. c	GP 1		16. d	GP 2
4. c	GP 2		17. a	GP 2
5. b	GP 2		18. a	GP 2
6. b	GP 4		19. d	GP 3
7. c	GP 4		20. b	GP 3
8. b	GP 3		21. a.	GP 3
9. a	GP 2		22. c	GP 3
10.a	GP 2		23. c	GP 1
11.b	GP 2		24. a	GP 2
12.b	GP 1		25. c	GP 4
13.d	GP 2			

CHAPTER 2: THEORY AND RESEARCH

This chapter introduces the basic theoretical issues and perspectives in the study of human development. Developmental research designs and the concept of ethics in the study of human development conclude this informative chapter. This annotated outline is helpful as a guide to important issues and concepts discussed in the chapter.

Guideposts for Study

1. What purposes do theories serve?

2. What are two basic theoretical issues on which developmental scientists differ?

3. What are five theoretical perspectives on human development, and what are some theories representative of each?

4. How do developmental scientists study people, and what are some advantages and disadvantages of each research method?

5. What ethical problems may arise in research on humans?

Detailed Chapter Outline with Key Terms

I. BASIC THEORETICAL ISSUES
   - **Theory**: Set of logically related concepts that seek to describe, explain, and predict behavior.
   - **Data**: Information gathered by research.
   - **Hypotheses**: Tentative explanations or predictions that can be tested by research.
   A. Issue 1: Is Development Active or Passive?
      - *Tabula rasa:* Literally, a "blank slate"; philosopher John Locke's view that society influences the development of the child.
      - **Mechanistic model**: Model that views people like machines that react to environmental input.
      - **Organismic model**: Model that views people as active, growing organisms that set their own development in motion.
   B. Issue 2: Is Development Continuous or Discontinuous?
      - *Quantitative change:* Changes in number or amount, such as height, weight, or size of vocabulary.
      - *Qualitative change:* Changes in kind, structure, or organization and is discontinuous.

II. THEORETICAL PERSPECTIVES
   A. Perspective 1: Psychoanalytic
      - **Psychoanalytic perspective**: View of development as shaped by unconscious forces that motivate human behavior.

- *Psychoanalysis:* A therapeutic approach aimed at giving patients insight into unconscious emotional conflicts.
1. Sigmund Freud: Psychosexual Development
   a. Freud proposed three hypothetical parts of the personality:
      - *Id:* Part of the personality that governs newborns, operating on the pleasure principle. (*Pleasure principle:* The drive to seek immediate satisfaction of needs and desires.)
      - *Ego:* Part of the personality that represents reason, operating on the reality principle. (*Reality principle:* Finding realistic ways to gratify the id.)
      - *Superego:* Part of the personality containing the conscience, incorporating socially approved behavior into the child's own value system.
   b. In Freudian theory, an unvarying sequence of stages of personality development during infancy, childhood, and adolescence, in which gratification shifts from the mouth to the anus and then to the genitals:
      - *Fixation:* In psychoanalysis, an arrest in development that can show up in adult personality.
      - *Oral stage:* Stage in psychosexual development in which feeding is the main source of sensual pleasure.
      - *Anal stage:* Stage in psychosexual development in which the chief source of pleasure is moving the bowels.
      - *Phallic stage:* Stage in psychosexual development in which boys develop sexual attachment to their mothers and girls to their fathers, with aggressive urges toward the same-sex parent.
        - *Oedipus Complex:* a boy's sexual attachment to his mother.
        - *Electra Complex:* a girl's sexual attachment to her father.
      - *Latency stage:* Stage in psychosexual development in which the child is sexually calm and becomes socialized, develops skills, and learns about self and society.
      - *Genital stage:* Stage in psychosexual development that lasts throughout adulthood, in which repressed sexual urges resurface to flow in socially approved channels.
2. Erik Erikson: Psychosocial Development
   Psychosocial Development: The socially and culturally influenced process of development of the ego, or self, which Erikson described in eight stages:
   - *Basic trust versus basic mistrust:* Critical theme of infancy, in which hope is developed.
   - *Autonomy versus shame and doubt:* Child develops a balance of independence and will.
   - *Initiative versus guilt:* Early childhood stage in which purposed is derived.
   - *Industry versus inferiority:* Child learns skills of the culture.
   - *Identity versus identity confusion:* Adolescent determines a sense of self.
   - *Intimacy versus isolation:* Young adult makes commitment to others.
   - *Generativity versus stagnation:* Mature adult establishes and guides the next generation.

- *Ego integrity versus despair:* Late adulthood stage in which one must come to terms with the way one has lived one's life or succumb to despair.
  B. Perspective 2: Learning
  - **Learning perspective**: View that development results from learning.
  - *Learning:* A long-lasting change in behavior based on experience or adaptation to the environment.
  1. Behaviorism
     - **Behaviorism**: A mechanistic theory that emphasizes the predictable role of environment in causing observable behavior.
     - *Associative learning:* The formation of a mental link between two events.
       a. **Classical Conditioning:** A response to a stimulus is evoked after repeated association with a stimulus that normally elicits it.
       b. **Operant conditioning**: Learning based on association between behavior and its consequences formulated by B. F. Skinner.
     - **Reinforcement**: The process of strengthening a behavior and increasing the likelihood that the behavior will be repeated.
     - **Punishment**: Process by which a behavior is weakened, decreasing the likelihood of repetition.
     - *Extinguished:* Term referring to the return of a behavior to its original, or baseline, level after removal of reinforcement.
     - *Behavior modification:* Also called behavior therapy, it is the use of conditioning to gradually eliminate undesirable behavior or to increase positive behavior.
  2. Social Learning (Social Cognitive) Theory
     - **Social learning theory**: Theory developed by Albert Bandura that learning is bidirectional and based upon reciprocal determinism.
     - **Reciprocal determinism**: concept that the person acts on the world as the world acts on the person.
     - **Observational learning** *(modeling):* Learning through watching others' behavior and seeing the consequences for that behavior.
     - *Social cognitive theory:* Bandura's newest version of social learning theory, in which the emphasis on cognitive response to perceptions is increased.
     - *Self-efficacy:* A confidence that a person has the characteristics needed to succeed.
  C. Perspective 3: Cognitive
  Cognitive perspective: View that focuses on thought processes and the behaviors that reflect those processes.
  1. Jean Piaget's Cognitive-Stage Theory
     Clinical method: Technique combining observation with flexible questioning.
     - **Organization**: The tendency to create categories by observing the characteristics of individual members of that category.
     - **Schemes**: Cognitive structures that organize information about the world.
     - **Adaptation**: How children handle new information in light of what they already know.

- **Assimilation**: Part of adaptation; taking in new information and incorporating into existing cognitive structures.
- **Accommodation**: Part of adaptation; changing one's cognitive structures to include new information.
- **Equilibration**: The constant striving for a stable balance in the shift from assimilation to accommodation.

2. **Lev Vygotsky's Sociocultural Theory**
   - **Sociocultural theory:** Vygotsky's view stresses active engagement resulting in a *collaborative* process.
   - **Zone of Proximal Development (ZPD:** The gap between what a person is already able to do and what they are not quite ready to accomplish by themselves.
   - **Scaffording:** the termporay support that parents, teachers, and others give a child in doing a task until the child can do it alone.

3. **Information-processing approach**: Approach in which cognitive development is studied by analyzing the processes involved in making sense of incoming information and performing tasks effectively.
   a. *Computational Model*: Flowcharts that analyze the specific steps people go through in gathering, storing, retrieving, and using information.

4. **Neo-Piagetian Theories:** Set of theories that are a blend of Piaget's concepts along with some processes from information processing theories.

D. Perspective 4: Contextual

   Contextual perspective: View of development that sees the individual as inseparable from the social context.

   1. Urie Bronfenbrenner's **Bioecological Theory**: Approach to understanding processes and contexts of development:
      - **Microsystem**: The everyday environment of home, school, work and other face-to-face relationships.
      - **Mesosystem**: Linkages between two or more microsystems.
      - **Exosystem**: Linkages between a microsystem and outside systems that do affect a person indirectly.
      - **Macrosystem**: A society's overall cultural patterns such as dominant beliefs, ideologies, and economic and political systems.
      - **Chronosystem**: The dimension of time: change and constancy in the person and the environment.

E. Perspective 5: Evolutionary/Sociobiological

   Evolutionary/sociobiological Perspective: E.O. Wilson's focus on the evolutionary and biological bases of behavior.
   - *Survival of the fittest:* Darwinian process in which the individual most capable of survival (the one with the most adaptable traits) survives to pass on his or her genes to offspring.
   - *Natural selection:* Darwinian process in which the weak and those with maladaptive traits are removed from the gene pool, leaving only the healthiest and strongest to survive and continue the species.
   - **Ethology**: Study of distinctive adaptive behaviors of species of animals.

- **Evolutionary psychology**: Application of Darwinian principles of natural selection and survival of the fittest to individual
  - **Developmental Systems Approach**: View that development is an outcome of a dynamic process of bidirectional interaction between person and environment.
  - **Evolutionary Development**: View that applies the evolutionary principles to child development.

F. A Shifting Balance

Emphases continually shifts with the current focus being more on biological bases of behavior.

- Bidirectional—the view that people change their world even as it changes them.

II. RESEARCH METHODS
- **Quantitative research**: Research that deals with measurable data.
- **Qualitative research**: Research that involves the interpretation of nonnumerical data.
- **Scientific method**: System of established principles and processes of scientific inquiry. The usual steps in the method are:
  1. *Identify a problem* to be studied.
  2. *Formulate hypotheses* to be tested by research.
  3. *Collect data.*
  4. *Analyze the data* to determine whether they support the hypothesis.
  5. *Form tentative conclusions*
  6. *Disseminate findings* so that other observers can check, learn from, analyze, repeat, and build on the results.

A. Sampling
- *Population:* A group to whom the findings in research may apply.
- **Sample**: A smaller group within the population.
- *Generalize:* Application of results from a sample study to the population as a whole.
- *Random selection:* Method of selecting participants in a study so that each person in a population has an equal and independent chance of being chosen.

B. Forms of Data Collection
1. Self-Reports: Diaries, Interviews, Questionnaires
- *Parental self-reports:* A log or record of activities kept by the parents of young children, concerning the children's activities.
- *Interview:* Method in which researchers, either face-to-face or on the telephone, ask questions about attitudes, opinions, or behavior.
- *Questionnaire:* Printed questions that participants fill out and return.
2. Naturalistic and Laboratory Observation
  - **Naturalistic observation**: Research method in which behavior is studied in natural or real-life settings without intervention or manipulation.
  - **Laboratory observation**: Research method in which all participants are observed under the same controlled conditions.
  - *Observer bias:* The researcher's tendency to interpret data to fit expectations or to emphasize some aspects and minimize others

3. Behavioral and Performance Measures
   - *Valid:* The test measure what it claims to measure.
   - *Reliable:* A test in which the results are reasonably consistent.
   - *Standardized:* A test that is given and scored by the same methods and criteria.
   - **Operational definitions**: Definitions stated solely in terms of the operations or procedures used to produce or measure a phenomenon.
   - **Cognitive neuroscience:** linking cognitive functioning with brain processes.

C. Basic Research Designs
   1. Case Studies
      Case study: Study of an individual.
   2. Ethnographic Studies
      - **Ethnographic study**: Method that seeks to describe the pattern of relationships, customs, beliefs, technology, arts, and traditions that make up a society's way of life.
      - **Participant observation**: A form of naturalistic observation in which researchers live or participate in the societies they observe, often for long periods on time.
   3. Corrclational Studies
      - **Correlational study**: Research design intended to discover whether a statistical relationship between variables exists.
      - *Correlation:* A statistical relationship between two or more variables.
      - *Variables:* Phenomena that change or vary among people or can be varied for purposes of research.
      - *Positive correlation:* Variables that are related increase or decrease together.
      - *Negative correlation:* Variables have an inverse relationship; as one increases, the other decreases.
   4. Experiments
      - **Experiment**: Rigorously controlled, replicable procedure in which the researcher manipulates variables to assess the effect of one on the other.
      - *Replicate:* Repeating an experiment in exactly the same way with different participants to verify the results and conclusions.
      a. Groups and Variables
         - **Experimental group**: People who are to be exposed to the experimental manipulation or treatment.
         - **Control group**: People who are similar to those in the experimental group but do not receive the experimental treatment.
         - *Treatment:* The phenomenon the researcher wants to study.
         - *Treatment groups:* Groups that receive one of the treatments under study.
         - **Independent variable**: In an experiment, the condition over which the experimenter has direct control.
         - **Dependent variable**: In an experiment, the condition that may or may not change as a result of changes in the independent variable.
      b. Random Assignment
         - *Random assignment:* Assigning the participants in an experiment to groups in such a way that each person has an equal chance of being placed in any group.

- *Confound:* Contamination of an experiment by unintended differences between the groups.
  c. Laboratory, Field, and Natural Experiments
     - *Laboratory experiments:* Experiment in which the participants are brought to a laboratory where they experience conditions manipulated by the experimenter.
     - *Field experiment:* A controlled study conducted in an everyday setting, such as home or school.
     - *Natural experiment:* Study comparing people who have been accidentally "assigned" to separate groups by circumstances of life and lacks the control of the laboratory or field experiment.
  D. Developmental Research Designs
     1. Longitudinal, Cross-Sectional, and Sequential Designs
        - **Cross-sectional study**: Study design in which people of different ages are assessed on one occasion.
        - **Longitudinal study**: Study designed to study the same person or group of people more than once, sometimes years apart.

        - **Sequential study**: Study design that combines cross-sectional and longitudinal techniques.
  E. Ethics of Research
     1. Ethical issues
        1. Informed Consent: consent freely given with full knowledge of what the research entails
        2. Avoidance of Deception:
        3. Protection from harm or loss of dignity
        4. Guarantee of Privacy and Confidentiality
        5. Right to decline or withdraw
        6. Responsibility of investigators to correct any undesirable effects
     2. Three principles in resolving ethical dilemmas
        1. *Beneficence:* obligation to maximize benefit and minimize harm.
        2. *Respect:* protection of participant's autonomy.
        3. *Justice:* include diverse groups with sensitivity to research.

True/False Self-Test

Place a T or an F in the space provided. These questions are taken from the chapter content, tables, key terms, Guideposts for Study, and Checkpoints.

1. _____ A theory is used to explain data and to generate hypotheses that can be tested by research.

2. _____ The psychoanalytic perspective sees development as motivated by unconscious emotional conflicts.

3. _F_   Freud described two stages of psychosocial development.

4. _F_   The learning perspective is concerned with hidden or unconscious behaviors.

5. _T_   Cognitive neuroscience uses brain imaging and the study of people with brain injuries to determine how the brain controls and influences behavior.

6. _F_   Association of fear with getting immunizations is an example of operant conditioning.

7. _T_   Piaget's theory includes four stages of increasingly complex cognition.

8. _T_   Bandura's social learning theory stresses observational learning and imitation of models.

9. _F_   Bronfenbrenner felt the microsystem was more important than the macrosystem.

10. _T_   Vygotsky's sociocultural theory focuses on interaction between the individual and social context.

11. _F_   The ethological perspective is represented by Piaget and Vygotsky.

12. _T_   Random selection of a research sample can ensure generalizability.

13. _T_   To arrive at sound conclusions, researchers use the scientific method.

14. _F_   Correlations can establish cause and effect relationships.

15. _F_   Laboratory experiments are difficult to control and replicate.

16. _F_   The learning perspective views people as fostering their own development through choice, creativity, and self-realization.

17. _F_   A child's home, parents, and siblings are considered the child's macrosystem according to Bronfenbrenner.

18. _T_   The ethological perspective focuses on biological and evolutionary bases of behavior.

19. _T_   Two kinds of associative learning are classical conditioning and operant conditioning.

20. _T_   Behaviorism is a mechanistic theory.

21. _T_   Erikson's crisis in infancy is trust versus mistrust and helps to develop hope.

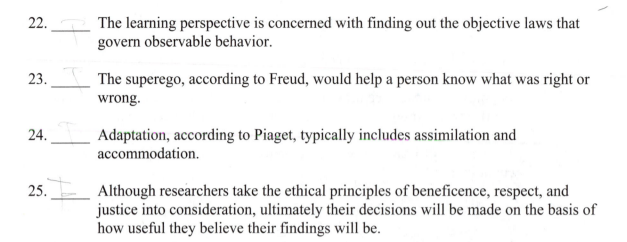

22. ___T___ The learning perspective is concerned with finding out the objective laws that govern observable behavior.

23. ___T___ The superego, according to Freud, would help a person know what was right or wrong.

24. ___T___ Adaptation, according to Piaget, typically includes assimilation and accommodation.

25. ___F___ Although researchers take the ethical principles of beneficence, respect, and justice into consideration, ultimately their decisions will be made on the basis of how useful they believe their findings will be.

Multiple-Choice Self-Test

Circle the letter of the best answer. These questions are based on many aspects of the chapter content, in no particular order.

1. The data collected in research is not protected and other people know who the participants were. This is a violation of the ethical principle of:
   a. loss of self esteem.
   b. confidentiality.
   c. informed consent.
   d. loss of dignity.

2. A set of logically related concepts or statements, which seeks to describe and explain human development, is a:
   a. case study.
   b. correlation.
   c. theory.
   d. hypothesis.

3. The model of human development that sees people as active, growing organisms that set their own development in motion is the _____ model.
   a. mechanistic
   b. psychosocial.
   c. behaviorist
   d. organismic

4. Research concerning the influences of heredity and environment on almost all characteristics has found that there is:
   a. a stronger genetic influence.
   b. an interaction between the two forces.
   c. a stronger environmental influence.
   d. None of these.

5. Mechanistic theorists see development as:
   a. developmentally based.
   b. characterized by quantitative change.
   c. always governed by the same processes.
   d. All of these.

6. The theoretical perspective that is concerned with the observable behavior of individuals is the _____ perspective.
   a. psychoanalytic
   b. ethological
   c. contextual
   d. learning

7. According to Freud, newborns are governed by:
   a. the id.
   b. the superego.
   c. the ego.
   d. None of these.

8. Erik Erikson developed a theory that included:
   a. eight stages across the life span.
   b. psychosocial development.
   c. lifelong ego development.
   d. All of these.

9. Learning theorists see development as:
   a. occurring in stages.
   b. qualitatively changing.
   c. continuous.
   d. impossible to define.

10. Behaviorism is:
    a. focused on associative learning.
    b. an organismic theory.
    c. experimental at this time.
    d. an information-processing tool.

11. Ivan Pavlov developed:
    a. a hierarchy of human needs.
    b. the principles of classical conditioning.
    c. social learning theory.
    d. bioecological theory.

12. According to social cognitive theory, children gradually develop a sense of:
a. self-actualization.
b. guilt.
c. self-efficacy.
d. transcendence.

13. Piaget's cognitive stage theory, the neo-Piagetian theories, and the information-processing approach are all part of the:
a. ethological perspective.
b. contextual perspective.
c. psychoanalytic view.
d. cognitive perspective.

14. Piaget's term for the way a child handles new information that seems to conflict with what the child already knows is:
a. adaptation.
b. organization.
c. schemes.
d. demarcation.

15. Dr. Smith studies how children model aggression from parents. This is an example of the _____ approach.
a. psychosexual
b. learning
c. social learning
d. cognitive

16. Sarah is learning about kittens and building an organized mental pattern of kittens. She is forming:
a. an id.
b. microsystems.
c. a superego.
d. schemes.

17. Bioecological theory was developed by:
a. Albert Bandura.
b. Sigmund Freud.
c. Urie Bronfenbrenner.
d. Erik Erikson.

18. According to bioecological theory, a system that includes personal, face-to-face relationships and bidirectional influences that flow back and forth is a:
a. mesosystem.
b. microsystem.
c. exosystem.
d. chronosystem.

19. Vygotsky differs from Piaget by seeing children as:
a. more passive.
b. unable to change.
c. fearful of the environment.
d. more engaged with the environment.

20. The simplest form of self-report is:
a. a questionnaire.
b. a diary or log.
c. an interview.
d. the Denver Developmental Screening Test.

21. The researcher's tendency to interpret data to fit expectations, or to emphasize some facts and minimize others, is known as:
a. quantification.
b. correlation.
c. observer bias.
d. naturalistic observation.

22. An in-depth study of a culture or subculture is known as a(n):
a. ethnographic study.
b. case study.
c. bioecological study.
d. experiment.

23. Laboratory experiments are:
a. generalized.
b. easy to control and replicate.
c. microgenetic studies.
d. ways to resolve ethical issues.

24. Dr. Yeh watches children at the university child development center. She is using a(n)
a. laboratory study.
b. field study.
c. ethological study.
d. correlational study.

25. A researcher is watching teenagers interact at a concert. He is using
a. naturalistic observation.
b. laboratory observation.
c. an experimental design.
d. Both a and b

Short Essay Questions

These short essay questions are based in part on the Checkpoints in the chapter. Answer each question as completely and succinctly as possible. Check your answers by reviewing the part of the chapter that covers the Guidepost listed with each question.

1. Discuss the three principles used to resolve ethical issues. (See Guidepost 5.)

2. Describe the five interlocking contextual systems proposed by Bronfenbrenner. (See Guidepost 3.)

3. List Piaget's stages of cognitive development and the key characteristics of thinking at each stage. (See Guidepost 3.)

4. Describe two types of observation and the advantages and disadvantages of each. (See Guidepost 4.)

5. What ethical problems may arise in research? (See Guidepost 5.)

Organize It!

Making lists helps organize information into easily recalled form. The following lists are based on the chapter content, Guideposts for Study, and Checkpoints.

1. List and briefly describe the two basic theoretical issues on which developmental scientists differ. (See Guidepost 2.)

   1.

   2.

2. List and describe three forms of data collection. (See Guidepost 4.)

   1.

   2.

   3.

3. List and describe four research designs (two qualitative and two quantitative) used to study child development. (See Guidepost 4.)

   1.

   2.

   3.

   4.

4. List and briefly describe the eight stages of Erikson's theory. (See Guidepost 3.)

   1.

   2.

   3.

   4.

   5.

   6.

   7.

   8.

5. List and describe Freud's five stages of psychosexual development. (See Guidepost 5.)

   1.

   2.

   3.

   4.

   5.

Critical Thinking Questions

These questions may be used in small group discussions or, if your instructor agrees, as extra-credit reports. Select an up-to-date journal article on development and answer the following questions.

1. After reading the article, identify the researchers' main hypothesis.

2. Identify the methods the researchers used to investigate their research questions.

3. If you were going to repeat this study, what would you change?

Answer Keys

True/False Self-Test

1. T	GP 1		14. F	GP 4
2. T	GP 3		15. F	GP 4
3. F	GP 3		16. F	GP 3
4. F	GP 3		17. F	GP 3
5. T	GP 3		18. T	GP 3
6. F	GP 3		19. T	GP 3
7. T	GP 3		20. T	GP 2
8. T	GP 3		21. T	GP 3
9. F	GP 3		22. T	GP 3
10. T	GP 3		23. T	GP 3
11. F	GP 3		24. T	GP 3
12. T	GP 4		25. F	GP 5
13. T	GP 4			

Multiple-Choice Self-Test

1. b	GP 5		14. a	GP 3
2. c	GP 1		15. c	GP 3
3. d	GP 2		16. d	GP 3
4. b	GP 2		17. c	GP 3
5. b	GP 2		18. b	GP 3
6. d	GP 3		19. d	GP 3
7. a	GP 3		20. b	GP 4
8. d	GP 3		21. c	GP 4
9. c	GP 3		22. a	GP 4
10. a	GP 3		23. b	GP 4
11. b	GP 3		24. a	GP 4
12. c	GP 3		25. a	GP 4
13. d	GP 3			

PART 2: BEGINNINGS

CHAPTER 3: FORMING A NEW LIFE

This chapter focuses on the mechanisms of heredity, the influences of heredity and environment, and on prenatal development. The issues of genetic testing and genetic engineering, and fetal welfare versus mothers' rights are addressed in the boxed features.

Guideposts for Study

1. How does conception normally occur and what causes multiple births?

2. How does heredity operate in determining sex and transmitting normal and abnormal traits?

3. How do scientists study the relative influences of heredity and environment, and how do heredity and environment work together?

4. What roles do heredity and environment play in physical health, intelligence, and personality?

5. What are the three stages of prenatal development, and what happens during each stage?

6. What environmental influences can affect prenatal development?

7. What techniques can assess a fetus's health, and why is prenatal care important?

Detailed Chapter Outline with Key Terms

I. CONCEIVING NEW LIFE
    A. How Fertilization Takes Place
        - **Fertilization**: Combining sperm and ovum to produce a zygote; also called *conception.*
        - *Gametes:* The sex cells, ovum and sperm.
        - **Zygote**: Single-celled organism resulting from fertilization.
        - *Follicle:* Small sac in the ovary containing the immature ova.
        - *Ovulation:* The rupture of a mature follicle and expulsion of the ovum.
        - *Cilia:* Tiny hair cells in the fallopian tubes that sweep the ovum along.
        - *Cervix:* The opening of the uterus.
    B. What Causes Multiple Births?
        - **Dizygotic (two-egg) twins**: Twins conceived by the union of two different ova with two different sperm cells; also called *fraternal twins.*
        - **Monozygotic (one-egg) twins**: Twins resulting from the division of a single zygote after fertilization; also called *identical twins.*
        - **Temperament**: Characteristic disposition or style of approaching and reacting to situations.
        - **Semi**-identical twins—the result of two sperm cells fusing with a single ovum.

II. MECHANISMS OF HEREDITY

Heredity: The inborn factors, inherited from the biological parents, that affect development.

A. The Genetic Code

- **Deoxyribonucleic acid (DNA)**: Chemical that carries inherited instructions for the formation and function of body cells.
- *Bases:* Chemical units that make up DNA; adenine, thymine, cytosine, and guanine.
- **Genetic code**: Sequence of base pairs within DNA, which determines inherited characteristics.
- **Chromosomes**: Coils of DNA that carry the genes.
- **Genes**: Small segments of DNA located in definite positions on particular chromosomes.
- **Human Genome:** The complete sequence of genes in the human body.
- *Meiosis:* Type of cell division in which each sex cell (gamete) ends up with only 23 chromosomes.
- *Mitosis:* Type of cell division in which each cell divides in half repeatedly, resulting in new cells with 46 chromosomes.

B. What Determines Sex?

- **Autosomes**: The 22 pairs of chromosomes not related to sexual expression.
- **Sex chromosomes**: Pair of chromosomes that determines sex: XX in the normal female, XY in the normal male.
- *X chromosomes:* Chromosomes containing the genes for femaleness.
- *Y chromosomes:* Chromosomes containing the genes for maleness.
- *Wnt-4:* A signaling molecule that appears to control the development of female characteristics.

C. Patterns of Genetic Transmission

1. Dominant and Recessive Inheritance

- **Alleles**: Genes that can produce alternative expression of a characteristic.
- **Homozygous**: Possessing two identical alleles for a characteristic.
- **Heterozygous**: Possessing differing alleles for a characteristic.
- **Dominant inheritance**: Pattern of inheritance in which a child receives matching dominant alleles, or when a child receives contradictory alleles. In either case, the dominant characteristic is expressed.
- **Recessive inheritance**: Pattern of inheritance in which a child receives identical recessive alleles, resulting in expression of a nondominant trait.
- **Polygenic inheritance**: Pattern of inheritance in which multiple genes affect a complex trait.
- **Mutations:** permanent alterations in genetic material that occur spontaneously or due to environmental hazards.

2. Genotypes and Phenotypes: Multifactorial Transmission

- **Phenotype**: Observable characteristics of a person.
- **Genotype**: Genetic makeup of a person, containing both expressed and unexpressed characteristics.
- **Multifactorial transmission**: Combination of genetic and environmental factors to produce certain complex traits.

3. Epigenesis: Environmental Influence on Gene Expression
Epigenesis or Epigenetic framework: Chemical molecules attached to a gene, which alter the way a cell "reads" the gene's DNA.
- Genetic imprinting: the differential expression of certain genetic traits, depending o whether the trait has been inherited from the mother or father.

D. Genetic and Chromosomal Abnormalities
1. Defects Transmitted by Dominant or Recessive Inheritance
Incomplete dominance: Partial expression of a trait.
2. Defects Transmitted by Sex-Linked Inheritance
- **Sex-linked inheritance**: Pattern of inheritance in which certain characteristics carried on the X chromosome inherited from the mother are transmitted differently to her male and female offspring.
- *Carrier:* Person who does not have an expressed genetic trait but can pass on the gene for it to offspring.
- **Natural selection:** failure of some individuals to survive and reproduce due to environmental demands.
3. Chromosomal Abnormalities
- **Down syndrome**: Chromosomal disorder characterized by moderate-to-severe mental retardation and by such physical signs as a downward-sloping skin fold at the inner corners of the eyes.
- *Trisomy-21:* Another name for Down syndrome, in which there is an extra 21st chromosome or a translocation of part of the 21st chromosome onto another chromosome.

E. Genetic Counseling and Testing
- **Genetic counseling**: Clinical service that advises couples of their probable risk of having children with hereditary defects.

III. NATURE AND NURTURE: INFLUENCES OF HEREDITY AND ENVIRONMENT
A. Studying Heredity and Environment
Behavioral genetics: Quantitative study of the influence of heredity and the environment upon specific traits.
1. Measuring Heritability
- **Heritability**: Statistical estimate of contribution of heredity to individual differences in a specific trait within a given population.
- *Family studies:* Study in which researchers measure the degree to which biological relatives share certain traits and whether the closeness of the familial relationship is associated with the degree of similarity.
- *Adoption studies:* Study in which researchers look at similarities between adopted children and their adoptive families, and also between adopted children and their biological families.
- *Studies of twins:* Study in which researchers compare pairs of monozygotic and same-sex dizygotic twins.
- **Concordant**: Term describing twins who share the same trait or disorder.
B. How Heredity and Environment Work Together
Developmental system: The combination of constitutional factors (those related to biological and psychological makeup) with social, economic, and cultural factors that help shape development.

1. Reaction Range and Canalization
   - **Reaction range**: Potential variability, depending on environmental conditions, in the expression of a hereditary trait.
   - *Norm of reaction:* Term used in the developmental system model in place of reaction range; the idea that the limits set by heredity are unknowable and their effects unpredictable because of the complexity of development.
   - **Canalization**: Limitation on variance of expression of certain inherited characteristics.
2. **Genotype-Environment Interaction**: The portion of phenotypic variation that results from the reactions of genetically different individuals to similar environmental conditions.
3. **Genotype-Environment Correlation** *(genotype-environment covariance)*: Tendency of certain genetic and environmental influences to reinforce each other; may be passive, reactive (evocative), or active.
   - *Passive correlations:* The parents, who provide the genes that predispose a child toward a trait, also tend to provide an environment that encourages development of that trait.
   - *Reactive, or evocative, correlations:* Children with differing genetic make-ups evoke different responses from adults.
   - *Active correlations:* Older children actively choose or create experiences consistent with their genetic tendencies.
   - **Niche-picking**: Tendency of a person, especially after early childhood, to select or create experiences consistent with that person's genetic tendencies.
4. What Makes Siblings Different? The Nonshared Environment
   Nonshared environmental effects: The unique environment in which each child grows up, consisting of distinctive influences or influences that affect one child differently than another.

C. Some Characteristics Influenced by Heredity and Environment
   1. Obesity:
      Obesity: Overweight, measured by body mass index
   2. Intelligence
   3. Personality and Psychopathology
      - **Temperament**: An aspect of personality that is largely inborn.
      - **Schizophrenia**: Neurological disorder marked by a loss of contact with reality; symptoms include hallucinations and delusions.

IV. PRENATAL DEVELOPMENT
   - Gestation: the approximately 9 month-period of development between conception and birth.
   - Gestational age: measurement of development from conception.
A. Stages of Prenatal Development
1. Germinal Stage (Fertilization to 2 Weeks)
   - **Germinal stage**: First 2 weeks of prenatal development, characterized by rapid cell division, increasing complexity and differentiation, and implantation in the wall of the uterus.
   - *Mitosis:* Period of rapid cell division and duplication.

- *Blastocyst:* A fluid-filled sphere of cells that will float into the uterus and implant in the lining.
- *Embryonic disk:* A thickened cell mass located on the blastocyst, from which the embryo begins to develop.
- *Ectoderm:* The upper layer of the embryonic disk that will form into the outer layer of skin, the nails, hair, teeth, sensory organs, and the nervous system.
- *Endoderm:* The lower layer of the embryonic disk that will form into the digestive system, liver, pancreas, salivary glands, and respiratory system.
- *Mesoderm:* The inner layer of the embryonic disk that will form into the inner layer of skin, muscles, skeleton, and excretory and circulatory systems.
- *Placenta:* Organ that provides oxygen and nourishment to the developing baby and removes its body wastes.
- *Umbilical cord:* Cord that connects the placenta to the baby and vice versa.
- *Amniotic sac or Amniotic cavity:* Fluid-filled membrane that encases the developing baby, protecting it and giving it room to move.
  - *Amnion and chorion:* Outer layers of amniotic sac.

2. Embryonic Stage (2 to 8 Weeks)
   - **Embryonic stage**: Second stage of gestation (2 to 8 weeks), characterized by rapid growth and development of major body systems and organs.
   - *Trimester:* A 3-month period of pregnancy.
   - **Spontaneous abortion**: Natural expulsion from the uterus of a conceptus that cannot survive outside the womb; also called *miscarriage.*
   - *Stillborn:* Term for a baby that is dead at its birth.

3. Fetal Stage (8 Weeks to Birth)
   - **Fetal stage**: Final stage of gestation (from 8 weeks to birth), characterized by increased detail of body parts and greatly enlarged body size.
   - **Ultrasound**: Prenatal medical procedure using high-frequency sound waves to detect the outline of a fetus and its movements, to determine whether a pregnancy is progressing normally.

B. Environmental Influences: Maternal Factors
   - **Teratogenic**: Capable of causing birth defects.
   - *Transforming growth factor alpha:* A variant of a growth gene, this factor causes a fetus to have six times more risk than other fetuses of developing a cleft palate if the mother smokes while pregnant.

1. Nutrition and Maternal Weight
2. Malnutrition
3. Drug Intake
   a. Medical Drugs
   b. Alcohol
      - **Fetal alcohol syndrome (FAS)**: Combination of mental, motor, and developmental abnormalities affecting the offspring of some women who consume alcohol during pregnancy.
   c. Nicotine
   d. Caffeine
   e. Marijuana, Cocaine, and Methamphetamine

4. Maternal Illness
  - **Acquired immune deficiency syndrome (AIDS)**: Viral disease that undermines functioning of the immune system.
  - **Perinatal transmission**: Virus may cross over to the fetus's bloodstream through the placenta during pregnancy, labor, or delivery or, after birth, through breast milk.
  - *Toxoplasmosis:* An infection caused by a parasite harbored in the bodies of cattle, sheep, pigs, and in the intestinal tracts of cats.
5. Maternal Stress and Anxiety
6. Maternal Age
7. Outside Environmental Hazards

C. Paternal Factors
D. Monitoring and Promoting Prenatal Development
  - *Sonogram:* A picture of the uterus, fetus, and placenta created by ultrasound directed into the mother's abdomen.
  - *Sonoembriology:* Technique in which high-frequency transvaginal probes and digital image processing are used to detect unusual defects during the embryonic stage.
  - *Embryoscopy, fetoscopy:* The insertion of a tiny viewing scope into a pregnant woman's abdomen to help detect nonchromosomal genetic disorders.
  - *Amniocentesis:* Technique in which a sample of the amniotic fluid, which contains fetal cells, is withdrawn and analyzed to detect genetic or other defects and chromosomal disorders.
  - *Chorionic villus sampling (CVS):* A technique in which tissue from the ends of the hairlike projections (villi) of the chorion are tested for the presence of birth defects and disorders.
  - *Preimplantation genetic diagnosis:* Technique in which embryos of four to eight cells, conceived by in vitro fertilization, are examined for defects before implantation.
  - *Umbilical cord sampling or fetal blood sampling:* Technique in which a needle is inserted into tiny blood vessels of the umbilical cord under the guidance of ultrasound to test fetal blood and deliver therapeutic measures.
  - *Maternal blood test:* Examination of a blood sample, taken from the mother between the 16th and 18th weeks of pregnancy, for the presence of alpha fetoprotein (AFP), an indicator of neural tube defects.

E. Disparities in Prenatal Care
F. The Need for Preconception Care

True/False Self-Test

Place a T or an F in the appropriate space. These questions are taken from the chapter content, tables, key terms, Guideposts for Study, and Checkpoints.

1. _____ Fertilization results in a single-celled organism called a zygote.

2. __F__ Dizygotic twins have the same genetic makeup.

3. __T__ Monozygotic twins are always of the same sex.

4. __T__ Differences in pre- and postnatal experiences may cause differences in the
personalities of identical twins.

5. __F__ The basic unit of heredity is the neuron.

6. __F__ Alcohol consumed by the mother during pregnancy is not known to have any
teratogenic effects.

7. __F__ At conception, each human being receives 46 chromosomes from each parent.

8. __T__ A child who receives an X chromosome from each parent will be genetically
female.

9. __T__ The male parent's chromosome determines the sex of the child.

10. __T__ The phenotype is a person's observable characteristics.

11. __F__ Most human characteristics are the result of a single gene.

12. __T__ Birth defects can be transmitted through simple dominant, recessive, or sex-linked
genes.

13. __F__ Down syndrome is an extremely rare chromosomal abnormality.

14. __T__ Through genetic counseling, prospective parents can receive information about the
mathematical odds of having children with certain birth defects.

15. __T__ Through genetic testing, certain birth defects like Tay-Sachs disease are on the
decline.

16. __T__ Monozygotic twins tend to have less variation within the developmental reaction
range than do dizygotic twins.

17 __T__ Siblings tend to be more different than alike in intelligence and personality.

18. __T__ Obesity is an example of a characteristic influenced by heredity and environment.

19. __F__ The gestation period for a human is 10½ months.

20. __F__ Growth and development both before and after birth are erratic and unpredictable.

21. __T__ More males are spontaneously aborted than females.

22. ___T___ Fetal activity can be observed via ultrasound.

23. ___F___ Postnatal care appears to be more important than prenatal care for the well-being of the baby.

24. ___T___ Nutrition, physical activity, smoking, and drinking are all important prenatal influences involving the mother.

25. ___T___ External influences in the environment may affect the father's sperm.

Multiple-Choice Self-Test

Circle the letter of the best answer. These questions are based on many aspects of the chapter content, in no particular order.

1. The process by which male and female gametes combine to form a single-celled zygote is known as:
   a. cloning.
   b. fertilization.
   c. meiosis.
   d. mitosis.

2. The rupture of a mature follicle and the expulsion of the ovum is known as:
   a. ovulation.
   b. intercourse.
   c. fertilization.
   d. menopause.

3. Dr. Brown is researching obesity among children who have been adopted, comparing the children's weights with those of their biological and adoptive parents. Dr. Brown is using the _____method.
   a. Family studies.
   b. Twin studies.
   c. Concordant studies.
   d. Adoption studies.

4. Fertilization takes place in the:
   a. ovaries.
   b. fallopian tube.
   c. cervix.
   d. uterus.

5. Susan seems to have a natural musical talent and chooses to spend her time with other musicians. This is an example of:
   a. The reaction range
   b. niche-picking
   c. canalization.
   d. All of these.

6. Fertilization is most likely if intercourse occurs:
   a. during the menstrual period.
   b. on the day after the menstrual period.
   c. on the day of ovulation or five days preceding ovulation.
   d. None of these.

7. Dizygotic twins occur when:
   a. one fertilized egg splits in two.
   b. two eggs are released and fertilized at the same time.
   c. one egg is fertilized by two sperm.
   d. None of these.

8. Monozygotic twins are:
   a. identical in genetic makeup.
   b. likely to be mirror images of each other in some physical characteristics.
   c. not always identical in temperament.
   d. All of these.

9. The incidence of multiple births in the United States:
   a. is declining rapidly.
   b. is rising rapidly.
   c. is unchanged in the last 50 years.
   d. is declining slightly

10. Jeff hears voices and has difficulty staying in touch with reality. He appears to have:
    a. autism.
    b. schizophrenia.
    c. depression.
    d. all of these.

11. Multiple births are:
a. more likely to lead to disability and death in infancy.
b. rising in the United States, partly as a result of delayed childbearing.
c. related to the increased use of fertility drugs.
d. All of these.

12. The developing organism is one week old and is attaching to the walls of the uterus. This is the _____ stage.
a. embryonic
b. fetal
c. germinal
d. mesodermic

13. Each gene is located by function in a definite position on the:
a. cell wall.
b. mitochondria.
c. chromosome.
d. cell.

14. The technique of removing fluid from around the developing fetus to test for genetic defects is known as:
a. amniocentesis.
b. metamorphosis.
c. Chorionic villus sampling.
d. embryoscopy.

15. Each sperm and each egg contains _____ chromosomes.
a. 23
b. 92
c. 46
d. 69

16. Sperm and egg are created through a cell-division process known as:
a. mitosis.
b. morphogenesis.
c. meiosis.
d. polygenesis.

17. The sex of the human baby is determined by the genetic contribution of the:
a. father.
b. mother.
c. paternal grandmother.
d. maternal grandmother.

18. Sara's pregnancy is at the 15th week. Her physician calls her baby a(n):
a. embryo.
b. fetus.
c. zygote.
d. ovum.

19. Genes that produce alternative expressions of a characteristic are:
a. clones.
b. homozygous.
c. alleles.
d. chromatophores.

20. The array of observable characteristics that expresses one's genetic makeup is known as:
a. genotype.
b. homozygous.
c. heterozygous.
d. phenotype.

21. Jen is in the 4th week of pregnancy and is told it is a critical time. She is in the _____ stage.
a. fetal
b. embryonic
c. zygotic
d. ovum

22. Defects such as Tay-Sachs disease are transmitted by:
a. dominant inheritance.
b. gene splicing.
c. recessive inheritance.
d. IVF.

23. Red-green color blindness and hemophilia are examples of genetic disorders that:
a. almost always appear in male children.
b. show up differently in male and female children.
c. are carried on the X chromosomes of an unaffected mother.
d. All of these.

24. The condition caused by an extra copy of chromosome 21 or by the translocation of a part of chromosome 21 onto another chromosome is:
a. Down syndrome.
b. Marfan syndrome.
c. Turner syndrome.
d. Klinefelter syndrome.

25. Prenatal development occurs in
a. six stages.:
b. four stages.
c. three stages.
d. 40 stages.

Short Essay Questions

These short essay questions are based on the Checkpoints in the chapter. Answer each question as completely and succinctly as possible. Check your answers by reviewing the part of the chapter that covers the Guidepost listed with each question.

1. Briefly describe the process of normal conception. When is the best time for intercourse if a couple wishes to have a child? (See Guidepost 1.)

2. Multiple births have increased significantly in the last decade in the United States. List and explain several possible reasons for this statistic. Base your answer on the chapter material. (See Guidepost 1.)

3. Compare and contrast the roles of heredity and environment in determining physical health, intelligence, and personality. (See Guidepost 3.)

4. Describe the ways in which environmental hazards may affect prenatal development. (See Guidepost 6.)

5. List the signs and symptoms of pregnancy. (See Table 3-4.)

Organize It!

Making a list is an easy way to remember clusters of related concepts, facts, and ideas. Below is a group of lists to make, based on Checkpoints in the chapter. Have fun!

1. List the three stages of prenatal development. Include one important feature of each. (See Guidepost 5.)

   1.

   2.

   3.

2. List and describe three methods of prenatal assessment and intervention. (See Guidepost 7.)

1.

2.

3.

3. List three maternal illnesses that have adverse effects on the embryo or fetus (See Guidepost 6.)

1.

2.

3.

4. List three ethnically-related genetic diseases and the ethnic group most at risk for each. (See Guidepost 2.)

1.

2.

3.

5. List four genetically-influenced psychopathological conditions (See Guidepost 4.)

1.

2.

3.

4.

6. List three kinds of influences that contribute to nonshared environmental effects. (See Guidepost 3.)

1.

2.

3.

Critical Thinking Questions

These questions can be used in small group discussions or, if your instructor agrees, for extra-credit reports.

1. Now that the human genome has been completed, how far do you think scientists and medical professionals should go in altering the genetic makeup of human beings? Consider these areas: eradication/correction of genetic diseases, gender selection, alteration of existing conditions such as vision defects or growth deficiencies, and physical trait selection.

2. Building on question 1, what are some potential benefits and problems with altering the genetic makeup of humans?

3. In what ways are you more like your mother, and in what ways are you more like your father? How are you similar or dissimilar to your siblings? How might these similarities and differences be influenced by heredity or environment?

4. How far should government go in protecting an unborn fetus from the pregnant mother's use of drugs and/or alcohol?

Answer Keys

True/False Self-Test

1.	T	GP 1		14.	T	GP 3
2.	F	GP 1		15.	T	GP 3
3.	T	GP 1		16.	F	GP 3
4.	T	GP 1		17.	T	GP 4
5.	F	GP 2		18.	T	GP 4
6.	F	GP 6		19.	F	GP 5
7.	F	GP 2		20.	F	GP 5
8.	T	GP 2		21.	T	GP 6
9.	T	GP 2		22.	T	GP 7
10.	T	GP 2		23.	T	GP 7
11.	F	GP 2		24.	T	GP 7
12.	T	GP 2		25.	T	GP 6
13.	F	GP 2				

Multiple-Choice Self-Test

1.	b	GP 1		14.	c	GP 7
2.	a	GP 1		15.	a	GP 2
3.	d	GP 2		16.	c	GP 2
4.	b	GP 3		17.	a	GP 5
5.	b	GP 3		18.	b	GP 2
6.	c	GP 3		19.	c	GP 2
7.	b	GP 1		20.	d	GP 2
8.	d	GP 1		21.	b	GP 5
9.	b	GP 1		22.	c	GP 2
10.	b	GP 4		23.	d	GP 2
11.	d	GP 5		24.	a	GP 2
12.	c	GP 5		25.	c	GP 5
13.	c	GP 2				

CHAPTER 4: PHYSICAL DEVELOPMENT IN THE FIRST THREE YEARS

The principles of early physical development are explored in depth in this informative chapter. The first part of the chapter focuses on birth and the newborn. The second part of the chapter explores early physical development, including brain development, reflex behaviors, and motor development.

Guideposts for Study

1. How has childbirth changed in developed countries?

2. How does labor begin, what happens during each of the three stages of childbirth, and what alternative methods of delivery are available?

3. How do newborn infants adjust to life outside the womb, and how can we tell whether a new baby is healthy and is developing normally?

4. What complications of childbirth can endanger newborn babies, and what are the prospects for infants with complicated births?

5. What factors affect infants' chances of survival and health?

6. What influences growth, and how do the brain and the senses develop?

7. What are the early milestones in motor development, and what are some influences on it?

Detailed Chapter Outline with Key Terms

I. CHILDBIRTH AND CULTURE: HOW BIRTHING HAS CHANGED
   A. Birth customs vary according to culture.
   B. 20th-century medical advances revolutionized birth in industrialized nations.
II. THE BIRTH PROCESS
   - *Labor:* Contractions of the uterus during childbirth.
   - **Parturition**: Process of uterine and cervical changes, usually lasting about two weeks, preceding childbirth.
   A. Stages of Childbirth
      - *First stage:* Usually the longest stage, may last 12 hours or more, in which regular and increasingly frequent uterine contractions widen or dilate the cervix.
      - *Second stage:* Lasting about 1½ hours, this stage begins when the baby's head moves through the cervix and into the vaginal canal, and ends when the baby emerges from the mother's body.
      - *Third stage:* Lasting only about 10 to 60 minutes, this stage is the expulsion of the placenta and remaining tissues from the uterus.
   B. Vaginal versus Cesarean Delivery
      - **Cesarean delivery**: Delivery of a baby by surgical removal from the uterus.
      - **Vaginal delivery**: Usual method of delivery.

C. Electronic Fetal Monitoring
- **Electronic Fetal Monitoring:** Mechanical monitoring of fetal heartbeat during labor or delivery.

D. Medicated versus Unmedicated Delivery
- **Natural or prepared childbirth**: Methods of childbirth developed by Dr. Dick-Read and Dr. Lamaze that seek to prevent pain by eliminating the mother's fear through education about the physiology of reproduction and training in breathing and relaxation during delivery.
- **Pedunal block**: local anesthesia used in delivery.
- **Epidural or spinal**: regional injections for anesthesia in delivery.
- *Doula*: An experienced helper that provides emotional support throughout labor.

III. THE NEWBORN BABY

Neonatal period: First 4 weeks of life, a time of transition from intrauterine dependency to independent existence.

A. Size and Appearance
- **Neonate**: Newborn baby, up to 4 weeks old.
- *Fontanels:* Places on a baby's head where the bones have not yet grown together.
- *Lanugo:* The birth hair, a fuzzy prenatal hair that will eventually drop off.
- *Vernix caseosa:* An oily protective covering against infection, which dries within the first few days and sloughs off.

B. Body Systems
- **Anoxia**: Lack of oxygen, which may cause brain damage.
- **Hypoxia**: a reduced oxygen supply.
- Meconium: Fetal waste matter, excreted during the first few days after birth.
- **Neonatal jaundice**: Condition, in many newborn babies, caused by immaturity of liver and evidenced by yellowish appearance.

C. Medical and Behavioral Assessment
  1. The Apgar Scare
  - **Apgar scale**: Standard measurement of a newborn's condition; it assesses appearance, pulse, grimace, activity, and respiration.
  2. Assessing Neurological Status: The Brazelton Scale
  - **Brazelton Neonatal Behavioral Assessment Scale (NBAS)**: Neurological and behavioral test to measure neonate's responses to the environment. It assesses:
    o Motor organization (such as activity level or motor coordination)
    o Reflexes
    o Attention and interactive capacities (such as general alertness and responsiveness)
    o Central nervous system instability (such as tremors and skin color changes)
  3. Neonatal Screening for Medical Conditions

D. States of Arousal

State of Arousal: An infant's physiological and behavioral status at a given moment in the periodic daily cycle of wakefulness, sleep, and activity.

IV. COMPLICATIONF OF CHILDBIRTH
A. Low Birthweight
  1. Low Birthweight

- **Low birthweight**: Weight of less than 5½ pounds (2,500 grams) at birth because of prematurity or being small for date.
- **Preterm (premature) infants**: Infants born before completing the 37th week of gestation.
- **Small-for-date (small-for-gestational age)**: Infants whose birthweight is less than that of 90 percent of babies of the same gestational age, as a result of slow fetal growth.
  a. How Many Babies Are Preterm, and Why?
      - Hydroxyprogesterone caproate or 17P: treatment for preterm babies
  b. How Many Babies are Low Birthweight, and Why?
  c. Who Is Likely to Have a Low-Birthweight Baby?
      - Demographic and socioeconomic factors
      - Medical factors predating pregnancy
      - Prenatal behavioral and environmental factors
      - Medical conditions associated with pregnancy

B. Immediate Treatment and Outcomes
   - *Very-low-birthweight babies:* Babies weighing less than 1,500 grams.
   - Isolette: an antiseptic, temperature-controlled crib
   - **Kangaroo care:** a method of skin-to-skin contact with infant
   - **Surfactant:** lung-coating substance that keeps the air sacs from collapsing and adding to survival.

C. Long-term Outcomes
   - *Extremely low-birthweight babies:* Babies weighing between 501 and 1,000 grams, or about 1 to 2 pounds

D. Postmaturity
   - **Postmature: baby born after 42 weeks.**

E. Stillbirth
   - **Stillbirth:** death of a fetus at or after the 20th week of gestation

F. Can a Supportive Environment Overcome Effects of Birth Complications?
   1. The Infant Health and Development Studies
   2. The Kauai Study
      Protective factors: Influences that reduce the impact of early stress and tend to predict positive outcomes including individual attributes, affectionate ties, and rewards at school, work, or place of worship.

V. SURVIVAL AND HEALTH
  A. Death During Infancy
      - **Infant mortality rate**: Proportion of babies born alive who die within the first year.
  1. Racial/Ethnic Disparities in infant mortality
  2. Sudden Infant Death Syndrome (SIDS)
      - **Sudden Infant Death Syndrome (SIDS):** Sudden and unexplained death of an apparently healthy infant and sometimes called crib death.
  3. Death from Injuries
  B. Immunization for Better Health

VI. EARLY PHYSICAL DEVELOPMENT

A. Principles of Development
- *Cephalocaudal principle:* Principle stating that growth (including sensory and motor development) occurs from the top down.
- *Proximodistal principle:* Principle stating that growth and motor development proceed from the center of the body outward.

B. Patterns of Growth

C. Nutrition
1. Breast or Bottle?
2. Encouraging Breastfeeding
2. Other Nutritional Concerns

D. The Brain and Reflex Behavior
- **Central nervous system**: Brain and spinal cord.
1. Building the Brain
   Brain growth spurts: periods of rapid growth and development that coordinate with cognitive changes
2. Major Parts of the Brain
   - *Brain stem:* The part of the brain responsible for such basic bodily functions as breathing heart rate, body temperature, and the sleep-wake cycle.
   - *Cerebellum:* The part of the brain that maintains balance and motor coordination.
   - *Cerebrum:* The largest part of the brain, divided into left and right hemispheres.
   - **Lateralization**: Tendency of each of the brain's hemispheres to have specialized functions.
   - *Corpus callosum:* A tough band of tissue joining the right and left hemispheres.
   - *Occipital lobe:* Section of the cerebral hemisphere that processes visual information.
   - *Parietal lobe:* Section of the cerebral hemisphere that processes touch and spatial information.
   - *Temporal lobe:* Section of the cerebral hemisphere that processes hearing and language.
   - *Frontal lobe:* Section of the cerebral hemisphere that permits high-level functioning such as speech and reasoning.
   - *Cerebral cortex:* The outer surface of the cerebrum.
3. Brain Cells
   - **Neurons**: Nerve cells.
   - *Glial cells:* Cells that support and protect the neurons.
   - *Axons:* Branching extension from the neuron that sends signals to other neurons.
   - *Dendrites:* Branching extensions from the neuron that receive incoming messages from other cells.
   - *Synapses:* Tiny gaps between neurons.
   - *Neurotransmitters:* Chemicals that bridge the synapse between neurons.
   - **Integration**: Process by which neurons coordinate the activities of muscle groups.
   - **Differentiation**: Process by which neurons acquire specialized structure and function.

- **Cell death**: Elimination of excess brain cells to achieve more efficient functioning.
4. Myelination
   - *Myelin:* Fatty substance that coats the neural pathways.
   - **Myelination**: Process of coating neurons with a fatty substance (myelin) that enables faster communication between cells.
   - *Hippocampus:* A structure deep in the temporal lobe that plays a key role in memory.
5. Early Reflexes
   - **Reflex behavior**: Automatic, involuntary, innate response to stimulation.
   - *Primitive reflexes:* Reflexes related to instinctive needs for survival and protection.
   - *Postural reflexes:* Reactions to changes in position or balance.
   - *Locomotor reflexes:* Reflexes that resemble voluntary movements that do not appear until months after the reflexes have disappeared, such as walking and swimming.
5. Molding the Brain: The Role of Experience
   - **Plasticity**: Modifiability, or "molding," of the brain through experience.
E. Early Sensory Capacities
   A. Touch and Pain
   B. Smell and Taste
   C. Hearing
   D. Sight
   Binocular vision: The use of both eyes to focus, allowing perception of depth and distance.
VII. Motor Development
   A. Milestones of Motor Development
      - **Systems of action**: Increasingly complex combinations of skills, which permit a wider or more precise range of movement and more control of the environment.
      - **Pincer grasp:** Grasp in which thumb and index finger meet at the tips to form a circle.
      - **Denver Developmental Screening Test**: Screening test given to children one month to six years old to determine whether they are developing normally.
      - **Gross motor skills**: Physical skills that involve the large muscles.
      - **Fine motor skills**: Physical skills that involve the small muscles and eye-hand coordination.
      1. Head Control
      2. Hand Control
      3. Locomotion
         - *Self-locomotion:* The ability of babies to get around under their own power by means of creeping or crawling.
         - *Social referencing:* infant looks to the caregiver for clues as to whether a situation is secure or frightening.
   B. Motor Development and Perception
      - **Visual guidance**: The use of the eyes to guide the movement of the hands (or

other parts of the body).
- **Depth perception**: Ability to perceive objects and surfaces three-dimensionally.
- **Haptic perception**: Ability to acquire information about properties of objects, such as size, weight, and texture, by handling them.

C. Eleanor and James Gibson's Ecological Theory
- **Visual cliff**: Apparatus designed to give an illusion of depth and used to assess depth perception in infants
- **Ecological theory of perception**: Theory developed by Eleanor and James Gibson, which describes developing motor and perceptual abilities as interdependent parts of a functional system that guides behavior in varying contexts.

D. How Motor Development Occurs: Thelen's Dynamic Systems Theory
- Walking reflex: stepping movements made by neonate
- **Dynamic Systems Theory (DST):** "Behavior emerges n the moment from the self-organization of multiple components." It is based on 4 principles: the element of time; the interaction of multiple causes; the integration of perception and cognition with action; and differing developmental pathways of individual children.

E. Cultural Influences on Motor Development

True/False Self-Test

Place a T or an F in the appropriate space. These questions are taken from the chapter content, tables, key terms, Guideposts for Study, and Checkpoints.

1. ___ Today, more than two-thirds of new mothers in the United States breastfeed.

2. ___ Breastfeeding may reduce the risks of SIDS.

3. ___ As of the year 2003, over 25% of births in the United States were by Cesarean section delivery

4. ___ The third stage of labor is typically the longest and may last over 12 hours.

5. ___ Shaken baby syndrome is easily diagnosed and almost always detected with follow-up calls to protective agencies.

6. ___ The Lamaze method of prepared childbirth help mothers cope with childbirth by providing increased medication to reduce pain.

7. ___ The brain is composed of two types of cells: neurons and glial cells.

8. ___ The fuzzy prenatal hair covering a newborn is called *vernix caseosa*.

9. ___ The average newborn weighs 8 to 9 pounds.

10. ___ The fetal waste matter is called meconium.

11. ___ Births in the United States today are as risky and dangerous as in the 19th century.

12. ___ A newborn that has an APGAR score of 9 would be characterized as medically healthy.

13. ___ Juan was born at 39 weeks weighing 4½ pounds. He is a small-for-date infant.

14. ___ Newborns prefer sour or bitter tastes over sweetness.

15. ___ Hearing is only functional after birth.

16. ___ Because Maria has previously had three miscarriages, she is considered to be a higher risk for subsequent pregnancies.

17. ___ The Denver Developmental Screening Test measures cognitive awareness.

18. ___ Development need not follow the same timetable in every child to reach the same destination.

19. ___ SIDS or Sudden Infant Death is more likely when a child is 18 months of age due to their greater mobility.

20. ___ The Kauai Study demonstrated that infant mortality can be reduced.

21. ___ African babies tend to be more advanced than American and European babies in sitting, walking, and running.

22. ___ Parents who are heavy smokers increase risks of infant mortality.

23. ___ Babies develop depth perception after 1 year of age.

24. ___ Walkers are considered dangerous by the American Academy of Pediatrics.

25. ___ The Brazelton Neonatal Behavioral Assessment Scale is used to assess responses to the environment and to predict future development.

Multiple-Choice Self-Test

Circle the letter of the best answer. These questions are based on many aspects of the chapter content, in no particular order.

1. The process of coating the neurons with a fatty substance is called:
   a. integration
   b. myelination
   c. differentiation
   d. plasticity

2. The changes that bring on labor typically begin about 2 weeks before delivery, as a result of:
   a. size of the baby.
   b. increased anxiety of the mother.
   c. the shifting balance of hormones.
   d. the size of the placenta.

3. Normal vaginal childbirth is accomplished in:
   a. six periods.
   b. three stages.
   c. seven stages.
   d. 40 stages.

4. The major changes in childbirth in developed countries are due to:
   a. birth in hospitals and care by a physician.
   b. birth at home and care by a midwife.
   c. birth under water with a midwife attending.
   d. birth at home with the father trained to deliver.

5. Cesarean delivery is a procedure that:
   a. is used to surgically deliver the baby.
   b. is no longer used.
   c. requires an episiotomy.
   d. is never required in the United States.

6. Advocates of natural childbirth argue that medicated birth:
   a. poses risks for the baby.
   b. deprives mothers of the empowering experience of childbirth.
   c. is not necessary with preparation.
   d. All of these.

7. Which of the following is true about settings for birth?
   a. Hospitals and doctors are by far the best option.
   b. Birth settings reflect the overall cultural system.
   c. Obstetricians agree that home births and midwives should be more strongly encouraged.
   d. They are regulated by the U.S. government.

8. Newborn Jacob would prefer which of the following tastes?
   a. sour
   b. bitter
   c. salty
   d. sweet

9. The layers of fat that develop during the last 2 months of gestation function to help newborns:
   a. roll over easily.
   b. appeal to their mothers.
   c. regulate body temperature.
   d. float in the bath.

10. A baby who is sleeping with eyes closed, with no eye movement, and cannot be aroused by mild stimuli is in the state of:
a. drowsiness.
b. alert inactivity.
c. irregular sleep.
d. regular sleep.

11. The Apgar Scale is used primarily for:
a. immediate assessment of the newborn.
b. fetal heart rate measurement.
c. behavioral assessment at 1 year.
d. weighing the newborn.

12. Babies who inherit the enzyme disorder phenylketonuria (PKU) will:
a. adjust within 1 month.
b. become jaundiced.
c. become mentally retarded unless placed on a special diet.
d. cry frequently at night.

13. Birth trauma may be caused by:
a. anoxia.
b. infection.
c. disease.
d. All of these.

14. Low-birth weight appears to be related to which of the following?
a. Lack of adequate nutrition.
b. Maternal tobacco use.
c. Maternal alcohol use.
d. All of these.

15. Postmature babies are typically:
a. long and thin.
b. at risk for death.
c. at risk for brain damage.
d. All of these.

16. In the United States, the leading cause of infant death is:
a. SIDS.
b. Respiratory Distress Syndrome (RDS).
c. birth defects.
d. low birthweight.

17. Which of the following is true of sudden infant death syndrome (SIDS)?
a. It is caused by choking.
b. Death occurs most often between 1 month and 4 months of age.
c. SIDS strikes only poor babies.
d. Only African American babies die of SIDS.

18. Growth and development before and after birth follows these two principles:
a. cephalocaudal and proximodistal.
b. body and brain.
c. Apgar and Brazelton.
d. All of these.

19. The best food for infants up to 1 year of age is:
a. cow's milk.
b. breast milk.
c. goat's milk.
d. iron-enriched formula.

20. Babies who are fed plain cow's milk in the early months may suffer from:
a. low carbohydrate intake.
b. iron-deficiency anemia.
c. Vitamin C deficiency.
d. Vitamin A deficiency.

21. A researcher is using a device that is called a visual cliff. That researcher is most probably studying:
a. visual guidance
b. haptic perception
c. depth perception
d. fine motor skills

22. An infant is kicking her legs and has learned to kick a toy to make a sound. She is building her:
   a. gross motor skills.
   b. fine motor skills.
   c. palmar grasping skills.
   d. pincer grasping skills.

23. The tendency for each of the brain's hemispheres to have specialized functions is called:
   a. differentiation
   b. lateralization
   c. plasticity
   d. systems of action

24. A pediatrician is using an assessment to measure a 3-year-old child's development. The assessment is most likely the:
   a. APGAR
   b. Brazelton Neonatal Assessment
   c. Denver Developmental Screening Test
   d. Cognitive Assessment of Skills.

25. Doctors suspect that a child's vision problem is due to a brain lobe abnormality. They will most likely be examining the child's _____ lobes of the brain.
   a. occipital
   b. parietal
   c. temporal
   d. frontal

Short Essay Questions

These short essay questions are based on the Checkpoints in the chapter. Answer each question as completely and succinctly as possible. Check your answers by reviewing the part of the chapter that covers the Guidepost listed with each question.

1. Summarize trends in infant mortality, and using those trends, explain why African American infants are less likely to survive than white infants. (See Guidepost 5.)

2. List risk factors for sudden infant death syndrome (SIDS). What is known about the causes, and prevention of SIDS? (See Guidepost 5.)

3. Explain why full immunization of all preschool children is important. (See Guidepost 5.)

4. Summarize pediatric recommendations regarding infant nutrition. Include in your summary breastfeeding versus formula; when to introduce cow's milk, solid foods, and fruit juices; and the most common nutritional deficiencies. (See Guidepost 4.)

5. Describe the changes in sleep patterns that occur during the first few months of life. Discuss the role of culture in influencing sleep patterns and arrangements. (See Guidepost 3.)

6. Summarize the development of the senses during infancy. (See Guidepost 6.)

7. What are the milestones of motor development during the first 3 years? Describe and give examples of several important influences on motor development. (See Guidepost 7.)

Organize It!

Making a list is an efficient and fun way to remember many types of information, including conceptual information. Once you have made your list, use it! Memorize it by singing it, saying it rhythmically, or dancing it into your memory. All of these methods put the information into your brain in easily recalled ways.

1. List the three stages of labor and one characteristic of each. (See Guidepost 2.)

    1.

    2.

    3.

2. List three distinctive features of a newborn baby. (See Guidepost 3.)

    1.

    2.

    3.

3. List three protective factors identified by the Kauai Study. (See Guidepost 5.)

    1.

    2.

    3.

4. List the five infant states of arousal and the characteristics of each. (See Guidepost 3.)

    1.

    2.

3.

4.

5.

5. Discuss the four principles of Thelen's Dynamic Systems Theory (DST). (See Guidepost 7)

    1.

    2.

    3.

    4.

5. List the five subtests of the Apgar Scale. (See Guidepost 3.)

    1.

    2.

    3.

    4.

    5.

6. List four factors that increase the likelihood that a woman will have an underweight or low-birthweight baby. (See Guidepost 4.)

    1.

    2.

    3.

    4.

7. List, in descending order, the four leading causes of infant deaths in the United States. (See Guidepost 5.)

    1.

    2.

    3.

    4.

8. List the five factors associated with the decrease in risks associated with pregnancy and childbirth over the past 50 years. (See Guidepost 1.)

    1.

    2.

    3.

    4.

    5.

Critical Thinking Questions

These questions may be used for small group discussions or research papers.

1. Should pregnant women who smoke, drink, take drugs, or take other actions that will hurt an unborn baby be held accountable in a court of law?

2. How far should parents go in trying to advance their infant's motor skills or cognitive skills?

Answer Keys

True/False Self-Test

1.	T	GP 6	14.	F	GP 6
2.	T	GP 6	15.	F	GP 6
3.	T	GP 2	16.	T	GP 4
4.	F	GP 2	17.	F	GP 7
5.	F	GP 5	18.	T	GP 7
6.	F	GP 2	19.	F	GP 5
7.	T	GP 6	20.	T	GP 5
8.	F	GP 3	21.	T	GP 5
9.	F	GP 3	22.	T	GP 5
10.	T	GP 3	23.	F	GP 6
11.	F	GP 1	24.	T	GP 5
12.	T	GP 3	25.	T	GP 3
13.	T	GP 4			

Multiple-Choice Self-Test

1.	b	GP 6	14.	d	GP 4
2.	c	GP 2	15.	d	GP 5
3.	b	GP 2	16.	c	GP 5
4.	a	GP 1	17.	b	GP 5
5.	a	GP 2	18.	a	GP 6
6.	c	GP 2	19	b	GP 6
7.	b	GP 2	20.	b	GP 7
8.	d	GP 6	21.	c	GP 7
9.	c	GP 4	22.	a	GP 6
10.	d	GP 3	23.	b	GP 6
11.	a	GP 3	24.	c	GP 7
12.	c	GP 3	25.	a	GP 6
13.	d	GP 4			

CHAPTER 5: COGNITIVE DEVELOPMENT DURING THE FIRST THREE YEARS

This chapter introduces classic, as well as newer, approaches to the study of cognitive development in early childhood. Language development is presented in depth in the second part of the chapter.

Guideposts for Study

1. What are six approaches to the study of cognitive development?

2. How do infants learn, and how long can they remember?

3. Can infants' and toddlers' intelligence be measured, and how can it be improved?

4. How did Piaget describe infants' and toddlers' cognitive development, and how well have his claims stood up?

5. How can we measure infants' ability to process information, and when do infants begin to think about characteristics of the physical world?

6. What can brain research reveal about the development of cognitive skills?

7. How does social interaction with adults advance cognitive competence?

8. How do babies develop language, and what influences contribute to linguistic progress?

Detailed Chapter Outline with Key Terms

I. STUDYING COGNITIVE DEVELOPMENT: SIX APPROACHES
   - **Behaviorist approach**: Approach to the study of cognitive development that is concerned with basic mechanics of learning.
   - **Psychometric approach**: Approach to the study of cognitive development that seeks to measure the quantity of intelligence a person possesses.
   - **Piagetian approach**: Approach to the study of cognitive development that describes qualitative stages in cognitive functioning.
   - **Information-processing approach**: Approach that focuses on perception, learning, memory, and problem solving.
   - **Cognitive neuroscience approach**: Approach that examines the nervous system.
   - **Social-contextual approach:** Approach that examines the impact of the environmental aspects on the learning process.
   A. Behaviorist Approach: Basic Mechanics of Learning
      1. Classical and Operant Conditioning
         - **Classical conditioning**: Learning based on associating a stimulus that does not ordinarily elicit a response with another stimulus that does elicit the response.
         - *Extinction:* The fading of classically conditioned learning that occurs when that learning is not reinforced.
         - **Operant conditioning**: Learning based on reinforcement or punishment.

2. Infant Memory

   Infantile amnesia: The inability to remember events that happened before the age of 3 years.

   Self recognition: The ability to know self in photographs and mirror.

B. Psychometric Approach: Developmental and Intelligence Testing

   - **Intelligent behavior**: Behavior that is goal-oriented and adaptive to circumstances and conditions of life.
   - **IQ (intelligence quotient) tests**: Psychometric tests that seek to measure intelligence by comparing a test-taker's performance with standardized norms.

   1. Testing Infants and Toddlers
      - **Developmental Tests:** measurements that compare a baby's performance with a large number of infants and toddlers at particular ages.
      - **Bayley Scales of Infant and Toddler Development**: Standardized test of infants' development in cognitive, language, motor, social-emotional, and adaptive behavior.

   2. Assessing the Impact of the Early Home Environment
      - **Home Observation for Measurement of the Environment (HOME)**: Checklist to measure home environment's influence on children's cognitive growth.

      Passive genotype-environment correlation: The interactions of both the genetic makeup of parents and the environment the parents provide.

   3. Early Intervention
      - **Early intervention**: Systematic process of providing services to help families meet young children's developmental needs.

C. Piagetian Approach: The Sensorimotor Stage

   Sensorimotor stage: In Piaget's theory, the first stage in cognitive development, during which infants learn through senses and motor activity.

   1. Substages of the Sensorimotor Stage
      - **Schemes**: Piaget's term for organized patterns of behavior used in particular situations.
      - **Circular reactions**: Piaget's term for processes by which an infant learns to reproduce desired occurrences originally discovered by chance.
        - *First substage (birth to about 1 month)*: Neonates begin to exercise some control over inborn reflexes, modifying and extending their schemes.
        - *Second substage (about 1 to 4 months)*: Babies learn to repeat a pleasant bodily sensation first achieved by chance (called a *primary circular reaction*).
        - *Third substage (about 4 to 8 months)*: Babies are interested in manipulating objects and engage in *secondary circular reactions*—intentional actions repeated not merely for their own sake but to get results beyond the infant's own body.
        - *Fourth substage, coordination of secondary schemes (about 8 to 12 months)*: Infants have learned to generalize from the past to solve new problems and exhibit complex, goal-directed behavior.
        - *Fifth substage (about 12 to 18 months)*: Infants experiment with new behavior to see what will happen. They engage in *tertiary circular reactions*—the varying of an action to get a similar result instead of mere repetition. Trial and error is used for problem solving.

> *Sixth substage, mental combinations (about 18 months to two years)*: A transition into the preoperational stage of early childhood.
2. Do Imitative Abilities Develop Earlier Than Piaget Thought?
   - **Invisible imitation**: imitation using parts of the body that a baby cannot see.
   - **Visible imitation**: imitation using the hands and feet, or parts of the body that the baby can see
   - **Deferred imitation**: Piaget's term for reproduction of an observed behavior after the passage of time by calling up a stored symbol of it.
   - **Elicited imitation**: imitation that is induced by researchers to a series of actions that the baby has never seen before.
3. Development of Knowledge about Objects and Space
   Object concept: The idea that objects have their own independent existence, characteristics, and location in space.
   a. When Does Object Permanence Develop?
      - **Object permanence**: Piaget's term for the understanding that a person or object still exists when out of sight.
3. Symbolic Development, Pictorial Competence, and Understanding of Scale
   - Symbols: intentional representations of reality.
   - Symbol-minded: attentive to symbols and their relationships to the things they represent
   - Pictorial competence: the ability to understand the nature of pictures.
   - Scale errors: momentary misperceptions of the relative sizes of symbolic and real objects.
   - **Dual representation hypothesis:** The ability for the child to represent both the object and the picture of the object simultaneously.
4. Evaluating Piaget's Sensorimotor Stage

D. Information-Processing Approach: Perceptions and Representations
   1. Habituation
      - **Habituation**: Simple type of learning in which familiarity with a stimulus reduces, slows, or stops a response.
      - **Dishabituation**: Increase in responsiveness after presentation of a new stimulus.
   1. Visual and Auditory Perceptual and Processing Abilities
      - **Visual preference**: Tendency of infants to spend more time looking at one sight than another.
      - *Novelty preference:* Tendency of infants to pay more attention to new stimuli than to familiar ones.
      - **Visual-recognition memory**: Ability to distinguish a familiar visual stimulus from an unfamiliar one when shown both at the same time.
      - **Cross-modal transfer**: Ability to use information gained by one sense to guide another.
      - *Joint attention or joint perceptual exploration:* responding to an adult's gaze by looking or pointing in the same direction.
   2. Information Processing as a Predictor of Intelligence
      - *Visual reaction time:* The measure of how quickly an infant's gaze will shift to a picture that has just appeared.

- *Visual anticipation:* The measure of how quickly an infant's gaze will shift to the place where the infant expects the next picture to appear.
- *Visual expectation paradigm:* Method of showing a series of computer-generated pictures briefly to an infant, some on the left and some on the right side of the infant's peripheral visual field.

3. Information Processing and the Development of Piagetian Abilities
- Categorization: Dividing the world into meaningful categories.
- Causality: The principle that one event causes another.
- **Violation-of-expectations**: Research method in which dishabituation to a stimulus that conflicts with experience is taken as evidence that an infant recognizes the new stimulus as surprising.
- *Innate learning mechanisms:* Reasoning abilities that may be present at an infant's birth.
- *Core Knowledge:* intuitive principles in the form of specialized brain modules that help infants organize their perceptions and experience.
  - *Conceptual understanding:* Understanding of the process.
  - *Perceptual awareness:* Awareness that something has happened but lacking understanding of concept.

E. Cognitive Neuroscience Approach: The Brain's Cognitive Structures
1. Memory Systems
- **Explicit memory**: Intentional and conscious memory, generally of facts, names, and events.
- **Implicit memory**: Unconscious recall, generally of habits and skills; sometimes called *procedural memory*.
- **Working memory**: Short-term storage of information being actively processing.
2. Understanding of Number
- *Prefrontal cortex:* The large portion of the frontal lobe directly behind the forehead, believed to control many aspects of cognition.

F. Social-Contextual Approach: Learning from Interactions with Caregivers
Guided participation: Participation of an adult and a child in an activity, in a manner that helps structure the activity and bring the child's understanding of it closer to an adult's.

II. LANGUAGE DEVELOPMENT
- **Language**: Communication system based on words and grammar.
A. Sequence of Early Language Development
Prelinguistic speech: Forerunner of linguistic speech; utterance of sounds that are not words.
1. Early Vocalization
- *Crying:* Newborn's means of communication; can signal hunger, sleepiness, or anger.
- *Cooing:* Squealing, gurgling, and making vowel sounds like "ahhh."
- *Babbling:* Repeating consonant-vowel strings, such as "ma-ma-ma-ma."
2. Perceiving Language Sounds and Structure
- *Phonemes:* Basic sounds of the child's native language.

3. Gestures
- *Conventional social gestures:* Gestures such as waving goodbye or nodding the head to signify "yes," taught to a child by an adult or older child.
- *Representational gestures:* Gestures that represent the desired action directly, such as holding an empty cup to one's mouth to signify wanting a drink.
- *Symbolic gestures:* Gestures that function much like words and are symbolic of the desired concept, such as blowing to mean hot or sniffing to mean flower.
4. First Words
- **Linguistic speech**: Verbal expression designed to convey meaning.
- **Holophrase**: Single word that conveys a complete thought.
- *Expressive:* Referring to spoken vocabulary.
- *Passive:* receptive or understood vocabulary
5. First Sentences
- **Telegraphic speech**: Early form of sentence consisting of only a few essential words.
- **Syntax**: Rules for forming sentences in a particular language.

B. Characteristics of Early Speech
- *Simplify:* Children use telegraphic speech to say just enough to get their meaning across.
- *Understand grammatical relationships they cannot yet express:* Although unable to string together enough words to express a complete action, children can understand action.
- *Underextend word meanings:* Certain words may be used by children to mean only a single object, but not other, similar objects.
- *Overextend word meanings:* Children will overgeneralize a word to objects that are only similar to the original referent.
- *Overregularize rules:* Children will apply rules rigidly, without recognizing exceptions, such as "mouses" instead of "mice."

C. Classic Theories of Language Acquisition: The Nature-Nurture Debate
- **Nativism**: Theory that human beings have an inborn capacity for language acquisition.
- **Language acquisitions device (LAD)**: In Chomsky's terminology, an inborn mechanism that enables children to infer linguistic rules from the language they hear.
- *Hand-babbling:* The gestures of deaf babies that are repeated over and over.

D. Influences on Early Language Development
1. Brain Development
- Brain stem and pons: The primitive parts of the brain and parts that are related to crying.
- Motor cortex: Part of the brain controlling movements of the face and larynx and related to babbling.
2. Social Interaction: The Role of Parents and Caregivers
a. Prelinguistic Period
b. Vocabulary Development
- **Code mixing**: Use of elements of two languages, sometimes in the same utterance, by young children in households where both languages are spoken.

- **Code switching**: Changing one's speech to match the situation, as in people who are bilingual.
  c. **Child-directed speech (CDS)**: Form of speech often used in talking to babies or toddlers; includes slow, simplified speech, a high-pitched tone, exaggerated vowel sounds, short words and sentences, and much repetition. Also called *parentese* or *motherese*.
3. Preparing for Literacy: The Benefits of Reading Aloud
- **Literacy:** The ability to read and write.
- *Describer style:* Adult style of reading to a child in which the adult focuses on describing what is going on in the pictures and invites the child to do so.
- *Comprehender style:* Adult style of reading to a child in which the adult encourages the child to look more deeply at the meaning of a story and to make inferences and predictions.
- *Performance-oriented style:* Adult style of reading to a child in which the reader reads the story straight through, introducing the main themes beforehand and asking questions afterward.
- *Dialogic or shared reading:* Shared reading in which the parent asks challenging questions and the child is encouraged to become the storyteller.

True/False Self-Test

Place a T or an F in the appropriate space. These questions are taken from the chapter content, tables, key terms, Guideposts for Study, and Checkpoints.

1. _____ The behaviorist approach to the study of intelligent behavior is concerned with measuring quantitative factors that make up intelligence.

2. _____ The Bayley Scales of Infant and Toddler Development is a widely used test that is an accurate predictor of later intelligence.

3. _____ Research using operant conditioning has found that infants' memory processes are much like those of older children and adults.

4. _____ Two types of learning that behaviorists study are classical conditioning and operant conditioning.

5. _____ Infants' memory of an action is closely linked to contextual clues.

6. _____ In normal infants, psychometric tests can indicate current functioning, but they are generally poor predictors of later intelligence.

7. _____ Parental responsiveness and the ability to create a stimulating home environment have been shown to be associated with cognitive development.

8. _____ The Piagetian approach is concerned with quantitative stages of cognitive development.

9. _____ According to Piaget, self-locomotion has no influence on the object concept.

10. ___ Research suggests that several abilities develop earlier than Piaget described.

11. ___ Deferred imitation, which Piaget placed in the last half of the 5th year, has been reported as early as 2 weeks.

12. ___ The information-processing approach is concerned with literacy skills.

13. ___ Indicators of the efficiency of infants' information processing include speed of habituation and dishabituation, visual preference, and cross-modal transfer.

14. ___ Violation-of-expectations research suggests that infants as young as 3½ to 5 months may have a rudimentary grasp of object permanence.

15. ___ Cognitive neuroscience researchers have found that some forms of implicit memory develop in the first few months of life.

16. ___ Explicit memory and working memory do not merge before 3 years of age.

17. ___ Neurological developments cannot explain the emergence of Piagetian skills and information-processing abilities.

18. ___ Through guided participation in play and other shared everyday activities, parents or caregivers help children learn the skills, knowledge, and values important in their culture.

19. ___ Babies use gestures such as pointing only after they have spoken their first word.

20. ___ A "naming explosion" typically occurs some time between 16 and 24 months of age.

21. ___ Children in households where two languages are spoken generally choose one language and stick to it.

22. ___ Telegraphic speech generally occurs between 18 and 24 months of age.

23. ___ Simplification, underextending and overextending word meanings, and overregularizing rules characterize early speech.

24. ___ Chomsky's nativistic theory maintains that children are born with a language acquisition device (LAD).

25. ___ Reading aloud to a child from an early age helps pave the way for literacy.

Multiple-Choice Self-Test

Circle the letter of the best answer. These questions are based on many aspects of the chapter content, in no particular order.

1. The behaviorist approach to the study of cognitive development is concerned with:
   a. the mechanics of learning.
   b. the quantitative factors that make up intelligence.
   c. predicting later intelligence from tests.
   d. qualitative stages of cognitive development.

2. According to the Home Observation for Measurement of Environment, two key factors in development are:
   a. television and art supplies.
   b. extended family status and socioeconomic status.
   c. education of the parents and type of community.
   d. parental responsiveness and the ability to create a stimulating home environment.

3. Piaget's sensorimotor stage, lasts from:
   a. 3 to 5 years.
   b. 5 to 7 years.
   c. birth to 2 years.
   d. 10 to 12 years.

4. Two year-old Molly is involved in an experiment where she is expected to use a model of a room to locate objects in the actual room. She has great difficulty with this task because she had not yet mastered:
   a. object permanence.
   b. dual representation.
   c. elicited imitation.
   d. spatial knowledge.

5. According to Piaget, children in the sensorimotor stage progress in cognitive and behavioral schemes in the following order:
   a. deferred imitation, problem solving, tertiary circular reaction
   b. tertiary circular reactions, secondary circular reactions, deferred imitation
   c. primary circular reactions, deferred imitation, secondary circular reactions
   d. primary, secondary, tertiary circular reactions, mental combinations

6. The efficiency of infants' information processing is indicated by:
   a. cross-modal transfer.
   b. object permanence.
   c. imitation.
   d. None of these.

7. Explicit memory and working memory emerge between what ages?
   a. 13 and 22 months
   b. 6 and 12 months
   c. 22 and 36 months
   d. 2 and 4 months

8. Children in households where two languages are spoken tend to do:
   a. better in one language than the other.
   b. poorly in school.
   c. code mixing and code switching.
   d. holophrasic speech until the age of 3.

9. Research into guided participation between parents and children in the United States and Argentina has documented that:
a. there are cultural variations in the influences of child rearing upon play.
b. parents in the United States stress autonomy.
c. Argentine parents stress social interdependence.
d. All of these.

10. Syntax and communicative abilities are fairly well developed in most children by the age of:
a. 2 years.
b. 1 year.
c. 18 months.
d. 3 years.

11. Early speech is characterized by:
a. underextending word meanings.
b. overextending word meanings.
c. overregularizing rules.
d. All of these.

12. The language acquisition device (LAD) is a key component of whose theory of language development?
a. Piaget
b. Chomsky
c. Vygotsky
d. Skinner

13. Child-directed speech:
a. crosses language barriers.
b. is not limited to spoken language.
c. helps children respond to emotional cues.
d. All of these.

14. The following is the expected sequence of language development:
a. babble, coo, holophrase
b. telegraphic speech, coo, babble
c. coo, babble, holophrase
d. holophrase, babble, coo

15. Young John says, "I thinked!" instead of "I thought." His speech is an example of:
a. overextending word meanings.
b. overregularization of rules.
c. underextending word meanings.
d. holophrasic speech.

16. Betsy's mother hands her a glass of milk, which Betsy does not want. She says, "No drink milk!" This is an example of:
a. telegraphic speech.
b. underextension of meanings.
c. theory of mind.
d. code mixing.

17. Six-month-old Jonathan sleeps through the loud playing of his siblings. This is an example of:
a. habituation.
b. classical conditioning.
c. operant conditioning.
d. information-processing failure.

18. Waving bye-bye, nodding the head to mean yes and no, and shaking the head to signify no are examples of:
a. nativist theory.
b. behaviorist theory.
c. conventional social gestures.
d. habituation.

19. Learning gestures before speech is:
a. a linguistic advantage.
b. an impediment in learning to speak.
c. something that should be discouraged.
d. not natural.

6. Summarize what studies of operant conditioning have shown about infant memory. (See Guidepost 2.)

Organize It!

Making a list is an easy way to categorize information into a unit that is readily recalled. Here are a few lists to make. You may want to add others of your own.

1. List the six substages of Piaget's sensorimotor stag. (See Guidepost 4.)

    1.

    2.

    3.

    4.

    5.

    6.

2. List the 7 conditions to foster competence that are incorporated in the HOME scales. (See Guidepost 2.)

    1.

    2.

    3.

    4.

    5.

    6.

    7.

3. List the brain structures responsible for implicit, preexplicit, explicit, and working memory. (See Guidepost 6.)

   1.

   2.

   3.

   4.

4. List five milestones of language development during the first three years. (See Guidepost 8.)

   1.

   2.

   3.

   4.

   5.

5. List five ways in which early speech differs from adult speech. (See Guidepost 8.)

   1.

   2.

   3.

   4.

   5.

6. List three examples of how parents or caregivers help babies learn to talk. (See Guidepost 8.)

   1.

   2.

   3.

Critical Thinking Questions

These questions may be used in small group discussions or as extra-credit reports, if your instructor allows extra-credit.

1.   What might be some drawbacks of early educational intervention programs?

2.   Much of Piaget's theory was developed from his observations of his own children as they grew from infancy to childhood. What are some advantages and disadvantages of this kind of observation?

3.   Using Piaget's research findings as a guide, what kind of toy would you buy for a child in each of Piaget's stages of cognitive development?

4.   Based on the findings concerning child-directed speech, is "baby talk" good or bad for babies? Why or why not?

Answer Keys

True/False Self-Test

1.	F	GP 1		14.	T	GP 5
2.	F	GP 3		15.	T	GP 6
3.	T	GP 2		16.	F	GP 6
4.	T	GP 2		17.	F	GP 6
5.	T	GP 6		18.	T	GP 7
6.	T	GP 3		19.	F	GP 8
7.	T	GP 3		20.	T	GP 8
8.	F	GP 4		21.	F	GP 8
9.	F	GP 4		22.	T	GP 8
10.	T	GP 4		23.	T	GP 8
11.	F	GP 4		24.	T	GP 8
12.	F	GP 5		25.	T	GP 8
13.	T	GP 5				

Multiple-Choice Self-Test

1.	a	GP 2		13.	d	GP 8
2.	d	GP 3		14.	c	GP 8
3.	c	GP 4		15	b	GP 8
4.	b	GP 4		16.	a	GP 8
5.	d	GP 4		17.	a	GP 5
6.	a	GP 5		18.	c	GP 8
7.	b	GP 6		19.	a	GP 8
8.	c	GP 8		20.	d	GP 8
9.	d	GP 7		21.	b	GP 2
10.	d	GP 8		22.	d	GP 4
11.	e	GP 8		23.	d	GP 8
12.	b	GP 8		24.	a	GP 7

CHAPTER 6: PSYCHOSOCIAL DEVELOPMENT DURING THE FIRST THREE YEARS

This chapter explores the development of trust, attachment, and the emerging sense of self in the first three years. Relationships with siblings, parents, and other children are presented in the second part of the chapter. The issues of early child care and parental employment are also discussed.

Guideposts for Study

1. When and how do emotions develop and how do babies show them?
2. How do infants show temperamental differences, and how enduring are those differences?
3. What roles do mothers and fathers play in early personality development?
4. When and how do gender differences appear?
5. How do infants gain trust in their world and form attachments, and how do infants and caregivers "read" each other's nonverbal signals?
6. When and how does the sense of self arise, and how do toddlers develop autonomy and standards for socially acceptable behavior?
7. How do infants and toddlers interact with siblings and other children?
8. How do parental employment and early child care affect infants' and toddlers' development?
9. What are the causes of child abuse and neglect, and what can be done about it?

Detailed Chapter Outline With Key Terms

I. FOUNDATIONS OF PSYCHOSOCIAL DEVELOPMENT
    - *Psychosocial development:* The interconnection of personality with social relationships.
    A. Emotions
        - **Emotions**: Subjective reactions to experience that are associated with physiological and behavioral changes.
        1. First Signs of Emotion
            a. Crying
                - *Hunger cry:* A rhythmic cry, not always associated with hunger.
                - *Angry cry:* A variation of the rhythmic cry in which excess air is forced through the vocal cords.
                - *Pain cry:* A sudden onset of loud crying without preliminary moaning, sometimes followed with holding the breath.
                - *Frustration cry:* Two or three drawn-out cries, with no prolonged breath-holding.
            b. Smiling and Laughing

Waking smiles: Voluntary smiles.
2. When Do Emotions Appear?
   a. Basic Emotions
   b. Emotions Involving the Self
      - **Self-conscious emotions**: Emotions such as embarrassment, empathy, and envy that require a degree of self-awareness.
      - **Self-awareness**: Realization that one's existence and functioning are separate from those of other people and things.
      - **Self-evaluative emotions**: Emotions such as pride, guilt, and shame that involve evaluation of one's own thoughts and behavior against socially appropriate thoughts and behavior.
   c. Empathy: Feeling What Others Feel
      - **Empathy**: The ability to put oneself in another person's place and feel what that person feels, or would be expected to feel, in a particular situation.
      - **Altruistic behavior**: acting out of concern for others with no expectation of reward.
3. Brain Growth and Emotional Development
   - *Cerebral cortex:* Outer covering of the brain where higher mental functions occur.
   - *Frontal lobes:* Front section of the cerebral cortex (one on each side of the brain), responsible in part for emotional responses.
   - *Limbic system:* Brain structure that is the seat of emotional reactions.
   - *Hippocampus:* Structure in the limbic system of the brain.
   - *Hypothalamus:* Structure of the brain involved in the limbic system and emotion.
   - *Sympathetic system:* Part of the autonomic nervous system that prepares the body for action—fight or flight.
   - *Parasympathetic system:* Part of the autonomic nervous system that in involved in excretion and sexual excitement.
B. **Temperament**: Characteristic disposition or style of approaching and reacting to situations.
   1. Studying Temperamental Patterns: The New York Longitudinal Study
      - **"Easy" children**: Children with a generally happy temperament, regular biological rhythms, and readiness to accept new experiences.
      - **"Difficult" children**: Children with irritable temperament, irregular biological rhythms, and intense emotional responses.
      - **"Slow-to-warm-up" children**: Children whose temperament is generally mild but who are hesitant about accepting new experiences.
   2. How Stable is Temperament?
   3. Temperament and Adjustment: "Goodness of Fit."
      - **Goodness of fit:** the match between a child's temperament and the environmental demands and constraints the child must deal with.
   4. Shyness and Boldness: Influences of Biology and Culture
      - *Inhibition to the unfamiliar:* Shyness, or how sociable a child is with strange children and how boldly or cautiously the child approaches unfamiliar objects and situations.
C. Earliest Social Experiences: The Infant in the Family

1. The Mother's Role
2. The Father's Role
3. Gender: How Different are Baby Boys and Girls?
   a. Gender Differences in Infants and Toddlers
   - **Gender**: What it means to be male or female.
   b. How Parents Shape Gender Differences
   - **Gender-typing**: Socialization process by which children, at an early age, learn appropriate gender roles.

II. DEVELOPMENTAL ISSUES IN INFANCY
   A. Developing Trust
   - **Basic trust versus basic mistrust**: Erikson's first stage in psychosocial development, in which infants develop a sense of the reliability of people and objects.
   - *Hope:* The belief of infants that they can fulfill their needs and obtain their desires.
   B. Developing Attachments
   Attachment: Reciprocal, enduring tie between infant and caregiver, each of whom contributes to the quality of the relationship.
   1. Studying Patterns of Attachment
      - **Strange Situation**: Laboratory technique used to study attachment.
      - **Secure attachment**: Pattern in which an infant cries or protests when the primary caregiver leaves and actively seeks out the caregiver upon his or her return.
      - *Secure base:* Infant's use of a parent or other familiar caregiver as a departure point for exploration and a safe place to return periodically for emotional support.
      - **Avoidant attachment**: Pattern in which an infant rarely cries when separated from the primary caregiver and avoids contact upon his or her return.
      - **Ambivalent (resistant) attachment**: Pattern in which an infant becomes anxious before the primary caregiver leaves, is extremely upset during his or her absence, and both seeks and resists contact on his or her return.
      - **Disorganized-disoriented attachment**: Pattern in which an infant, after separation from the primary caregiver, shows contradictory behaviors upon his or her return.
   2. How Attachment Is Established
   3. Alternative Methods to Study Attachment
   4. The Role of Temperament
   5. Stranger Anxiety and Separation Anxiety
      - **Stranger anxiety**: Wariness of strange people and places, shown by some infants during the second half of the first year.
      - **Separation anxiety**: Distress shown by an infant when a familiar caregiver leaves.
   6. Long-Term Effects of Attachment
   7. Intergenerational Transmission of Attachment Patterns
      Adult Attachment Interview (AAI): A semistructured interview that asks adults to recall and interpret feelings and experiences related to their childhood attachments.
   C. Emotional Communication with Caregivers: Mutual Regulation
   - **Mutual regulation**: Process by which infant and caregiver communicate emotional states to each other and respond appropriately.

- **"Still-face" paradigm**: Research method used to measure mutual regulation in infants 2 to 9 months old.
  D. **Social Referencing**: Understanding an ambiguous situation by seeking out another person's perception of it.
III. DEVELOPMENTAL ISSUES IN TODDLERHOOD
- *Sense of self:* The development of the toddler's knowledge of being a separate person from those around him or her.
- *Autonomy:* Self-determination.
- *Socialization:* Learning society's standards of behaviors.
- *Internalization of behavioral standards:* The toddler's tendency to make the behavioral standards of others, such as parents, a part of the toddler's mental structures and memories.
  A. The Emerging Sense of Self
  - **Self-concept**: Sense of self; descriptive and evaluative mental picture of one's abilities and traits.
  - *Personal agency:* Realization by infant that he or she can control external events.
  - *Self-*coherence: The sense of being a physical whole with boundaries.
  - *Self-awareness:* Conscious knowledge of the self as a distinct, identifiable being.
  B. Development of Autonomy
  - **Autonomy versus shame and doubt**: Erikson's second stage in psychosocial development, in which children achieve a balance between self-determination and control by others.
  - *Will:* virtue that develops in the stage of autonomy versus shame and doubt.
  - *Negativism:* The tendency of a toddler to shout "No!" just for the sake of resisting authority.
  C. The Roots of Moral Development: Socialization and Internalization
  - **Socialization**: Development of habits, skills, values, and motives shared by responsible, productive members of a society.
  - **Internalization**: Process by which children accept societal standards of conduct as their own; fundamental to socialization.
    1. Developing Self-Regulation
    - **Self-regulation**: Child's independent control of behavior to conform to understood social expectations.
    - *Attentional processes:* The ability to pay attention to stimuli.
    2. Origins of Conscience: Committed Compliance
    - **Conscience**: Internal standards of behavior, which usually control one's conduct and produce emotional discomfort when violated.
    - **Committed compliance**: Kochanska's term for wholehearted obedience of a parent's orders without reminders or lapses.
    - **Situational compliance**: Kochanska's term for obedience of a parent's orders only in the presence of signs of ongoing parental control.
    3. Factors in the Success of Socialization
    - *Moral emotions:* Emotions such as guilt and empathy.
    - *Moral conduct:* Responding to temptations to break rules and violate standards of behavior.

- *Moral cognition:* response to moral dilemmas.
- **Receptive Cooperation:** A child's eager willingness to cooperate harmoniously with a parent.

IV. CONTACT WITH OTHER CHILDREN
    A. Siblings
    B. Sociability With Nonsiblings

V. CHILDREN OF WORKING PARENTS
    A. Effects of Maternal Employment
    B. Early Child Care
        1. Factors in Impact of Child Care
        2. The NICHD Study: Isolating Child Care Effects

VI. MALTREATMENT: ABUSE AND NEGLECT
- *Maltreatment:* Deliberate or avoidable endangerment of a child.
- **Failure to Thrive:** neglect that results in poor growth

    A.   Maltreatment: Facts and Figures

- **Physical Abuse:** Injury to the body through punching, beating, kicking, or burning.
- **Neglect:** Failure to meet a child's basic needs.
- **Sexual Abuse:** Sexual activity or sexual touching involving a child and an older person.
- **Emotional Maltreatment:** acts of abuse or neglect that may cause behavioral, cognitive, emotional, or mental disorders.

    B. Contributing Factors: An Ecological View
        1.   Characteristics of Abusive and Neglectful Parents and Families
        2.   Community Characteristics and Cultural Values
    C. Helping Families in Trouble
    D. Long-term Effects of Maltreatment

True/False Self-Test

Place a T or an F in the appropriate space. These questions are taken from the chapter content, tables, key terms, Guideposts for Study, and Checkpoints.

1. _____ Crying, smiling, and laughing are reflexes, not emotions.

2. _____ Complex emotions seem to develop from earlier, simpler ones.

3. _____ The repertoire of basic emotions seems to be universal, but there are cultural variations in their expression.

4. _____ Children all fall into one category of temperament.

5. _____ Temperamental patterns appear largely to be inborn and are generally stable, but can be modified by experience.

6. _____ There are very few differences in child-raising practices worldwide.

7. ____ In most cultures, mothers, even when employed outside the home, provide more infant care than fathers.

8. ____ Mothers and fathers in some cultures have different styles of play with babies.

9. ____ Significant gender differences appear before infancy.

10. ___ Parents begin gender-typing boys and girls almost from birth.

11. ___ Erikson's first crisis of personality is autonomy versus shame and doubt.

12. ____ Attachment to fathers occurs much later than attachment to mothers.

13. ___ Separation anxiety and stranger anxiety do not appear until the age of 3 years.

14. ___ Researchers gauge mutual regulation by the still-face paradigm.

15. ___ Separation anxiety and stranger anxiety are no longer considered to be components of attachment.

16. ___ The Adult Attachment Interview can predict the security of a child's attachment on the basis of the parent's memories of her or his own childhood attachment.

17. ___ The belief that babies, after about the age of 6 months, show social referencing has been documented through research.

18. ___ The self-concept begins to emerge at the age of 3 years.

19. ___ The community, culture, the abuser, and the family all interact to contribute to the presence or absence of child maltreatment.

20. ___ Negativism is a normal manifestation of the shift from external control to self-control.

21. ___ Mothers' workforce participation during their children's first three years seems to have little or no impact on their children's development.

22. ___ High-quality day care may offset insensitive mothering.

23. ___ Self-awareness is demonstrated when recognizing oneself in the mirror.

24. ___ A child with a generally happy temperament, regular biological rhythms, and a readiness to accept new experiences is known as an "easy child."

25. ___ Spanking is a cultural factor that increases the risk of physical abuse.

Multiple-Choice Self-Test

Circle the letter of the best answer. These questions are based on many aspects of the chapter content, in no particular order.

1. Around the age of _____, most infants are intensely preoccupied with their principal caregivers, may become afraid of strangers, and tend to act subdued in new situations.
   a. birth to 3 months
   b. 6 to 9 months
   c. 9 to 12 months
   d. 18 to 36 months

2. Infants begin to play "social games" and try to get responses from people at the age of:
   a. 6 to 9 months.
   b. 9 to 12 months.
   c. 12 to 18 months.
   d. 3 to 6 months.

3. The first and most powerful way that infants communicate their needs is through:
   a. laughing.
   b. smiling.
   c. crying.
   d. eye contact.

4. A cry characterized by two or three drawn-out cries, with no prolonged breath-holding, is a:
   a. hunger cry.
   b. pain cry.
   c. angry cry.
   d. frustration cry.

5. A cry characterized by sudden onset with no preliminary moaning, sometimes followed by holding the breath, is a:
   a. basic hunger cry.
   b. pain cry.
   c. frustration cry.
   d. angry cry.

6. Babies indicate their emotions by:
   a. facial expression.
   b. motor activity.
   c. body language.
   d. All of these.

7. Emotions such as embarrassment, empathy, and envy arise:
   a. before the development of self-awareness.
   b. in early infancy.
   c. after the development of self-awareness.
   d. between 3 and 6 months of age.

8. The fourth cognitive shift in brain organization comes at:
   a. birth.
   b. age 1.
   c. age 2.
   d. age 3.

9. Self-awareness and self-conscious emotions develop during the:
   a. 1st year.
   b. 2nd year.
   c. 5th year.
   d. 8th year.

10. The New York Longitudinal Study is considered:
a. invalid today.
b. the pioneering study on temperament.
c. a foundation study of motor skill.
d. a conclusive study of day care.

11. A child who has mildly intense reactions, both positive and negative, responds slowly to novelty and change, and gradually develops liking for new stimuli after repeated, unpressured exposures is a(n)
a. easy child.
b. difficult child.
c. slow-to-warm-up child.
d. None of the above.

12. Research evidence points to the idea that temperament is:
a. unpredictable.
b. stable, inborn, and largely hereditary.
c. totally influenced by environment.
d. unstable in early childhood.

13. In China, children who exhibit shyness and inhibition are:
a. considered immature.
b. considered incompetent.
c. rejected by their mothers.
d. socially approved.

14. In Canada, children who exhibit shyness and inhibition are:
a. considered immature.
b. socially approved.
c. considered well-behaved.
d. None of these.

15. Harlow's research with monkeys showed that:
a. feeding is not the most important thing babies get from their mothers.
b. mothering includes the comfort of close body contact.
c. Both of these.
d. Neither of these.

16. According to Erikson, the crisis of trust versus mistrust:
a. includes a definite critical period.
b. is similar to imprinting.
c. forms immediately after birth.
d. continues until about 18 months of age.

17. Measurable differences between baby boys and girls are:
a. few.
b. many and varied.
c. well established.
d. None of these.

18. Overall, fathers are:
a. more talkative than mothers.
b. less talkative, negative, and supportive in their speech than mothers.
c. more involved with toddlers than mothers.
d. less likely than mothers to promote gender-typing.

19. According to Erikson, the critical element the development of basic trust is:
a. consistent feeding.
b. the sex of the baby.
c. the age of the mother.
d. sensitive, responsive, consistent caregiving.

20. A baby who cries when the mother leaves and greets her happily when she returns is displaying:
a. ambivalent attachment.
b. secure attachment.
c. avoidant attachment.
d. None of these.

21. A baby who does not cry when the mother leaves and avoids her when she returns is displaying:
a. avoidant attachment.
b. secure attachment.
c. ambivalent attachment.
d. disorganized-disoriented behavior.

22. Researchers measure attachment by:
a. what happens when the researcher leaves.
b. what happens when the caregiver returns.
c. how long the baby cries.
d. None of these.

23. Compared to those with other attachment patterns, securely attached toddlers are:
a. more sociable with peers.
b. more sociable with unfamiliar adults.
c. Both of these.
d. Neither of these.

24. The pediatrician states that a baby is not gaining weight due to neglect. The child suffers from:
a. Failure to thrive.
b. Child abuse.
c. Neglectful supervision.
d. Emotional maltreatment.

25. As infants and preschoolers, children with severely or chronically depressed mothers tend to be:
a. securely attached.
b. insecurely attached.
c. ambivalent-avoidant.
d. None of the above.

Short Essay Questions

These short essay questions are based on the Checkpoints in the chapter. Answer each question as completely and succinctly as possible. Check your answers by reviewing the part of the chapter that covers the Guidepost listed with each question.

1. Discuss the role of temperament and goodness of fit in the success of socialization. (See Guidepost 2.)

2. In view of Kochanska's research on the roots of conscience, what questions would you ask about the early socialization of antisocial adolescents and adults, whose consciences appear to be severely underdeveloped? (See Guidepost 6.)

3. Compare the roles of fathers and mothers, and compare parenting practices in at least two cultures. Include a comparison of the cultural differences in the ways fathers play with their babies. (See Guidepost 3.)

4. Describe long-term behaviors that are influenced by early attachment patterns. (See Guidepost 5.)

5. Describe the different types of child maltreatment. (See Guidepost 9.)

Organize It!

Making lists is a fun and useful way to categorize information in your mind. After making each list, think of ways to memorize it so that you have immediate recall. Singing a list, dancing while you recite it, or simply saying it in a rhythmic pattern as you are walking, driving, or jogging allows your brain to store the information in easily retrievable form. Try it!

1. List and briefly describe the three categories of children's temperament. (See Guidepost 2.)

    1.

    2.

    3.

2. List five criteria for good child care. (See Guidepost 8.)

    1.

    2.

    3.

    4.

    5

3. List and describe nine aspects of temperament identified by the New York Longitudinal Study. (See Guidepost 2.)

    1.

    2.

    3.

    4.

    5.

    6.

    7.

8.

9.

4. Discuss two cultural factors that increase the risk of abuse and neglect. (See Guidepost 9.)

    1.

    2.

Critical Thinking Questions

These questions may be used for small group discussions or research papers.

1. Based on the information about temperament in the text, do you think that it is best for parents of a shy child to accept the child's shyness or to try to change it?

2. Fathers are becoming more and more active in their roles as parents today. Despite this, many people feel that mothers will always be more important to babies and young children than fathers. Do you agree or disagree? Why or why not?

3. What ethical problems might exist in research using the Strange Situation?

4. Should parents place infants under one year of age in day care? Why or why not?

Answer Keys

True/False Self-Test

1.	F	GP 1		14.	T	GP 5
2.	T	GP 1		15.	T	GP 5
3.	T	GP 1		16.	T	GP 5
4.	F	GP 2		17.	F	GP 5
5.	T	GP 2		18.	F	GP 5
6.	F	GP 3		19.	T	GP 9
7.	T	GP 3		20.	T	GP 6
8.	T	GP 3		21.	T	GP 8
9.	F	GP 4		22.	T	GP 8
10.	T	GP 4		23.	T	GP 6
11.	F	GP 5		24.	T	GP 2
12.	F	GP 5		25.	F	GP 9
13.	F	GP 5				

Multiple-Choice Self-Test

1.	c	GP 3		14.	a	GP 2
2.	a	GP 1		15.	c	GP 5
3.	c	GP 1		16.	d	GP 5
4.	d	GP 1		17.	a	GP 4
5.	b	GP 1		18.	b	GP 3
6.	d	GP 1		19.	d	GP 5
7.	c	GP 1		20.	b	GP 2
8.	d	GP 1		21.	a	GP 2
9.	b	GP 5		22.	b	GP 5
10.	b	GP 2		23.	c	GP 5
11.	c	GP 2		24.	a	GP 9
12.	b	GP 2		25.	b	GP 5
13.	d	GP 2				

PART 3: EARLY CHILDHOOD

CHAPTER 7: PHYSICAL AND COGNITIVE DEVELOPMENT IN EARLY CHILDHOOD

This chapter introduces the student to normal physical and cognitive development from 3 to 6 years. Body growth and change, sleep patterns, and motor skills are discussed in the first part of the chapter. The preoperational child and cognitive development are explored in the second part of the chapter.

Guideposts for Study

1. How do children's bodies and brains change between ages 3 and 6, and what sleep problems and motor achievements are common?

2. What are the major health and safety risks for young children?

3. What are typical cognitive advances and immature aspects of preschool children's thinking?

4. What memory abilities expand in early childhood?

5. How is preschoolers' intelligence measured, and what are some influences on it?

6. How does language improve during early childhood, and what happens when its development is delayed?

7. What purposes does early childhood education serve, and how do children make the transition to kindergarten?

Detailed Chapter Outline with Key Terms

PHYSICAL DEVELOPMENT
I. ASPECTS OF PHYSICAL DEVELOPMENT
   A. Bodily Growth and Change
   B. Sleep Patterns and Problems
   - *Sleep or night terror:* The abrupt awakening of a child or adult from deep sleep in a state of panic, usually about one hour after falling asleep. The person typically remembers nothing about the episode in the morning.
   - **Enuresis**: Repeated urination in clothing or in bed.
   C. Brain Development
   D. Motor Skills
   - **Gross motor skills**: Physical skills that involve the large muscles.
   - **Fine motor skills**: Physical skills that involve the small muscles and eye-hand coordination.
   - **Systems of action**: Increasingly complex combinations of skills, which permit a wider or more precise range of movement and more control of the environment.
   1. **Handedness**: Preference for using a particular hand.

2. Artistic Development
- *Scribble:* In the first stage of children's artistic development, the vertical and zigzag lines drawn in patterns by young children.
- *Shapes:* Circles, squares, triangles, and other figures drawn by young children in the second stage of artistic development.
- *Designs:* combination of shapes into complex arrangements.
- *Pictorial:* The stage of artistic development in which children draw actual depictions of objects, such as houses and trees.

II. HEALTH AND SAFETY
  A. Nutrition: Preventing Obesity
  B. Malnutrition
  C. Deaths and Accidental Injuries
  D. Health in Context: Environmental Influences
    1. Socioeconomic Status and Race/Ethnicity
    2. Homelessness
    2. Exposure to Smoking: Air Pollution, Pesticides, and Lead

COGNITIVE DEVELOPMENT

III. PIAGETIAN APPROACH: THE PREOPERATIONAL CHILD
Preoperational stage: In Piaget's theory, the second major stage of cognitive development, in which children become more sophisticated in their use of symbolic thought but are not yet able to use logic.
  A. Advances of Preoperational Thought
    1. **Symbolic function**: Piaget's term for ability to use mental representations (words, numbers, or images) to which a child has attached meaning.
- *Deferred imitation:* Imitation of an action at a later time, based on a mental representation of the observed action.
- *Pretend play:* Play involving imaginary people or situations, also called *fantasy play, dramatic play, or imaginary play*.
- *Language:* The use of a system of symbols (words) to communicate.
    2. Understanding of Objects in Space
    3. Understanding of Causality
    Transduction: In Piaget's terminology, a preoperational child's tendency to mentally link particular experiences, whether or not a logical causal relationship exists.
    4. Understanding of Identities and Categorization
- *Identities:* The concept that people and many things are basically the same even if they change in form, size, or appearance.
- **Animism**: Tendency to attribute life to objects that are not alive.
    5. Understanding of Number
- *Ordinality:* The concept of *more* or *less, bigger* or *smaller*.
- *Cardinality:* The principle of counting.
- *Number sense*
  - o Counting (cardinality)
  - o Number knowledge (ordinality)
  - o Number transformation (simple addition and subtraction.
  - o Estimation

    o Number patterns
B. Immature Aspects of Preoperational Thought
  • **Centration**: In Piaget's theory, tendency of preoperational children to focus on one aspect of a situation and ignore others.
  • **Decenter**: In Piaget's terminology, to think simultaneously about several aspects of a situation.
  1. **Egocentrism**: Piaget's term for inability to consider another person's point of view.
  2. **Conservation**: Piaget's term for awareness that two objects that are equal according to a certain measure remain equal in the face of perceptual alteration so long as nothing has been added to or taken away from either object.
    • **Irreversibility**: Piaget's term for a preoperational child's failure to understand that an operation can go in two or more directions.
    • *Focus on successive states:* In Piaget's theory, the tendency for preoperational children to focus on the end states rather than the transformations from one state to another.
C. Do Young Children Have Theories of Mind?
  Theory of mind: Awareness and understanding of mental processes.
  1. Knowledge about Thinking and Mental States
    Social cognition: Ability to understand that others have mental states and to judge their feelings and intentions.
  2. False Beliefs and Deception
  3. Distinguishing between Appearance and Reality
  4. Distinguishing between Fantasy and Reality
  5. Influences on Individual Differences in Theory-of-Mind Development
D. Information-Processing Approach: Memory Development
  • **Encoding**: Process by which information is prepared for long-term storage and later retrieval.
  • **Storage**: Retention of memories for future use.
  • **Retrieval**: Process by which information is accessed or recalled from memory storage.
  • **Sensory memory**: temporary "holding tank" for incoming sensory information.
  • **Working memory**: a short term "storehouse" for information a person is actively working on, trying to understand, remember, or think about.
  • **Executive function**: the conscious control of thoughts, emotions, and actions to accomplish goals or solve problems.
  • **Central executive**: model of memory that states a part of the brain makes decisions about what is encoded into long term memory or not.
  • **Long-term memory**: a "storehouse" of virtually unlimited capacity.
  1. Recognition and Recall
    • **Recognition**: Ability to identify a previously encountered stimulus.
    • **Recall**: Ability to reproduce material from memory.
  2. Forming and Retaining Childhood Memories
    • **Generic memory**: Memory that produces scripts of familiar routines to guide behavior.

- **Script**: General remembered outline of a familiar, repeated event, used to guide behavior.
- **Episodic memory**: Long-term memory of specific experiences or events, linked to time and place.
- **Autobiographical memory**: Memory of specific events in one's own life.
3. Influences on Memory Retention
- **Social Interaction Model:** view that children collaborate with parents and adults and construct autobiographical memories.
4. Influence of Culture
E. Intelligence: Psychometric and Vygotskian Approaches
1. Traditional Psychometric Measures
- **Stanford-Binet Intelligence Scale**: Individual intelligence test used to measure memory, spatial orientation, and practical judgment.
- **Wechsler Preschool and Primary Scale of Intelligence, Revised (WPPSI-R)**: Individual intelligence test for children ages 3 to 7, which yields verbal and performance scores as well as a combined score.
2. Influences on Measured Intelligence
3. Testing and Teaching Based on Vygotsky's Theory
- *Dynamic testing:* A test based on Vygotsky's theory that measures potential abilities by giving a child leading questions, examples, and demonstrations that may help the child master a task.
- **Zone of Proximal Development (ZPD):** The gap between what a child is able to do and what they are not quite ready to accomplish by themselves.
- **Scaffolding:** temporary support provided by adults and teachers until child masters the task.
F. Language Development
1. Vocabulary
Fast mapping: Process by which a child absorbs the meaning of a new word after hearing it once or twice in conversation.
2. Grammar and Syntax
3. Pragmatics and Social Speech
- **Pragmatics**: Practical knowledge needed to use language for communication.
- **Social speech**: Speech intended to be understood by a listener.
- **Private speech**: Talking aloud to oneself with no intent to communicate.
4. Delayed Language Development
5. Preparation for Literacy
- **Emergent literacy**: Preschooolers' development of skills, knowledge, and attitudes that underlie reading and writing.
G. Early Childhood Education
1. Goals and Types of Preschools
- *Child-initiated:* A preschool in which the child actively directs his or her own learning experience.
- *Academically directed:* A preschool in which the focus is on the subject matter and teachers direct learning.

- *Middle-of-the-road:* A blend of the child-initiated and academically directed types of preschools.
2. Compensatory Preschool Programs
3. The Child in Kindergarten

True/False Self-Test

Place a T or an F in the appropriate space. These questions are taken from the chapter content, tables, key terms, Guideposts for Study, and Checkpoints.

1. ____ Compared to earlier periods, physical growth accelerates between the ages of 3 and 6.

2. ____ Girls are larger than boys throughout childhood.

3. ____ For their weight, preschool children eat less than they do in infancy and toddlerhood, but the prevalence of obesity during early childhood has increased.

4. ____ Sleep patterns are affected by cultural expectations.

5. ____ Sleep terrors tend to occur within an hour after falling asleep.

6. ____ Enuresis (bed-wetting) is common and is usually outgrown without special help.

7. ____ Handedness reflects dominance by one hemisphere of the brain.

8. ____ Stages of art production appear to reflect personality rather than brain development.

9. ____ Accidents are the leading cause of death during childhood in the United States.

10. ____ Preventable disease is no longer a problem in the developing world.

11. ____ Most fatal nonvehicular accidents occur at home.

12. ____ Minor illnesses help build immunity to disease.

13. ____ Environmental factors, such as exposure to stress, have no effect on the risk of illness or injury.

14. ____ Children in the preoperational stage of cognitive development always show maturity of thought.

15. ____ The symbolic function enables children to reflect on people, objects, and events only when they are present.

16. ____ Preoperational children can understand the concept of identity.

17. ___ Centration, or the inability to decenter, prevents preoperational children from understanding principles of conservation.

18. ___ The theory of mind occurs after age 12.

19. ___ Preoperational children are capable of empathy.

20. ___ Preoperational children often focus on states rather than transformations.

21. ___ Children become less competent in pragmatics as they engage in social speech.

22. ___ Interaction with adults can promote emergent literacy.

23. ___ At all ages, recall is better than recognition.

24. ___ Autobiographical memory is linked with the development of language.

25. ___ Children are less likely to remember unusual activities that they actually participate in.

Multiple-Choice Self-Test

Circle the letter of the best answer. These questions are based on many aspects of the chapter content, in no particular order.

1. Homeless families are typically headed by:
   a. senior citizens.
   b. single mothers.
   c. single fathers.
   d. adolescents.

2. Many poor children do not receive the medical care they need because:
   a. their parents are irresponsible.
   b. they are too healthy.
   c. they are uninsured.
   d. they have behavior problems.

3. Which of the following is true of homeless preschoolers?
   a. They are three times more likely than other children to lack immunizations.
   b. They suffer more health problems than other children.
   c. They experience high rates of diarrhea and tooth decay.
   d. All of these.

4. Advances of preoperational thought include:
   a. a growing understanding of identities.
   b. an ability to spell.
   c. an ability to do geometric and algebraic math problems.
   d. focusing on one aspect of a situation.

5. Marie lists which of her classmates are "nice" and which are "mean." She says, "The nice ones are all my friends." Marie is demonstrating:
   a. empathy.
   b. understanding of cause and effect.
   c. ability to classify.
   d. theory of mind.

6. Jeffrey cries when his father gives him a cookie that is broken in half. Because each half is smaller than the whole cookie, Jeffrey thinks he is getting less. Jeffrey is demonstrating:
   a. egocentrism.
   b. centration.
   c. animism.
   d. transductive reasoning.

7. Marie thinks clouds are alive because they move. She is demonstrating:
   a. theory of mind.
   b. centration.
   c. egocentrism.
   d. animism.

8. Thinking of something in the absence of sensory or motor cues, such as Wang Yani did when she painted from memory, is known as:
   a. the symbolic function.
   b. fine motor skills.
   c. irreversibility.
   d. centration.

9. The awareness of having experienced a particular incident that occurred at a specific time and place is known as:
   a. generic memory.
   b. episodic memory.
   c. script.
   d. None of these.

10. Autobiographical memory and the decline of childhood amnesia may be linked to:
    a. generic memory.
    b. age of the parents.
    c. development of language.
    d. vividness of an event.

11. The fourth edition of the Stanford-Binet IQ Test provides:
a. a single, overall measure of intelligence.
b. assessment of patterns and levels of cognitive development.
c. separate verbal and performance scores.
d. None of these.

12. Handedness is usually evident by age:
a. 3.
b. 6.
c. 8.
d. 10.

13. Which of the following is true about preventable diseases?
a. This group includes common colds.
b. They are no longer a problem worldwide.
c. They are rare today because of worldwide immunization.
d. They remain a major problem in the developing world.

14. The environmental influences that increase a child's risk of illness and injury include:
a. homelessness.
b. smoking.
c. poverty.
d. All of these.

15. The symbolic function is shown in:
a. egocentrism.
b. pretend play.
c. centration.
d. animism.

16. Which of the following can preoperational children generally NOT do?
a. understand classification
b. understand principles of counting
c. distinguish reality from fantasy
d. make fairly accurate judgments about spatial relationships

17. The existence of imaginary companions in the lives of children aged 3 to 10 is:
a. disturbing and should be investigated.
b. normal.
c. a desperate bid for attention.
d. a sign of intense stress.

18. Who is most likely to have an imaginary companion?
a. girls
b. boys
c. preverbal children
d. later-born children

19. The temporary support provided to help a child master a task is called:
a. scaffolding.
b. pragmatics.
c. fast mapping.
d. a social interaction model.

20. A child thinks she caused a window to break because she was playing with the light switch when a ball came through the window. This is an example of _____reasoning.
a. deductive
b. logical
c. symbolic
d. transductive

21. Children use imaginary companions to:
a. provide support in difficult situations.
b. provide wish fulfillment mechanisms.
c. be scapegoats.
d. All of these.

22. The process of "fast mapping" allows young children to:
a. find their way home from school.
b. increase their vocabulary rapidly.
c. enhance spatial abilities.
d. All of these.

23. Private speech is:
a. a sign of autism.
b. a sign of nervousness.
c. normal and common in childhood.
d. a speech problem.

24. The development of skills and knowledge that underlie reading and writing is known as:
a. phonics.
b. morphemes.
c. emergent literacy.
d. theory of mind.

25. _____ memory begins at about age 2 and produces a script.
a. Generic
b. Episodic
c. Semantic
d. Procedural

Short Essay Questions

These short essay questions are based on the Checkpoints in the chapter. Answer each question as completely and succinctly as possible. Check your answers by reviewing the part of the chapter that covers the Guidepost listed with each question.

1. Who should be responsible for children's well-being when parents cannot provide adequate food, clothing, shelter, and health care: government, religious and community institutions, the private sector, or a combination of these? Why? (See Guidepost 2.)

2. List some of the factors that contribute to the rising prevalence of obesity in preschoolers. What suggestions can you make for preventing it? (See Guidepost 2.)

3. What are the main motor achievements of early childhood? (See Guidepost 1.)

4. List and describe at least two examples of research that challenges Piaget's views on young children's cognitive limitations. (See Guidepost 4.)

5. Explain why preoperational children have trouble with conservation tasks involving two glasses of different shapes that each hold the same amount of water. (See Guidepost 4.)

6. Compare and discuss Piaget's "three mountains task" and Hughes's "doll and police officer task" in terms of theory and results. (See Guidepost 4.)

Organize It!

Making lists is a fun and useful way to categorize information in your mind. After making each list, think of ways to memorize it so that you have immediate recall. Singing a list, dancing while you recite it, or simply saying it in a rhythmic pattern as you are walking, driving, or jogging allows your brain to store the information in easily retrievable form. Try it!

1. List and briefly describe the three types of childhood memory. (See Guidepost 4.)

    1.

    2.

    3.

2. List and describe three ways that preschoolers increase their vocabularies. (See Guidepost 6.)

    1.

    2.

    3.

3. List and briefly describe the seven limitations of preoperational thought, according to Piaget. (see Table 7-4 and Guidepost 4.)

    1.

    2.

    3.

    4.

    5.

    6.

4. List eight ways to help a child get to sleep. (See Table 7-3 and Guidepost 1.)

   1.

   2.

   3.

   4.

   5.

   6.

   7.

Critical Thinking Questions

These questions may be used in small group discussions or as extra-credit reports. (Remember that extra credit assignments are completely up to the discretion of your instructor.)

1. What are some of the ways that television promotes poor nutrition for children?

2. How far should the government go in protecting children from their own parents?

3. Should teachers be permitted to know a child's IQ score? Should parents be told the score? Should the child be told the score? What are some implications of telling each of these individuals?

4. Do we place children in educational settings too early? Why or why not?

Answer Keys

True/False Self-Test

1.	F	GP 1
2.	F	GP 1
3.	T	GP 1
4.	T	GP 1
5.	T	GP 1
6.	T	GP 1
7.	T	GP 1
8.	F	GP 3
9.	T	GP 2
10.	F	GP 2
11.	T	GP 2
12.	T	GP 2
13.	F	GP 2
14.	F	GP 3
15.	F	GP 3
16.	T	GP 3
17.	T	GP 3
18.	F	GP 3
19.	T	GP 3
20.	T	GP 3
21.	F	GP 6
22.	T	GP 6
23.	F	GP 4
24.	T	GP 4
25.	F	GP 4

Multiple-Choice Self-Test

1.	b	GP 2
2.	c	GP 2
3.	d	GP 2
4.	a	GP 3
5.	c	GP 3
6.	b	GP 3
7.	d	GP 3
8.	a	GP 3
9.	b	GP 4
10.	c	GP 4
11.	b	GP 5
12.	a	GP 1
13.	d	GP 2
14.	d	GP 3
15.	b	GP 3
16.	c	GP 3
17.	b	GP 3
18.	a	GP 3
19.	a	GP 5
20.	d	GP 4
21.	d	GP 5
22.	b	GP 6
23.	c	GP 6
24.	c	GP 6
25.	a	GP 4

CHAPTER 8: PSYCHOSOCIAL DEVELOPMENT IN EARLY CHILDHOOD

This chapter introduces the various aspects of psychosocial development: the developing self, gender differences, play, parenting, and relationships with siblings and other children.

Guideposts for Study

1. How does the self-concept develop during early childhood, and how do children show self-esteem, emotional growth, and initiative?

2. How do boys and girls become aware of the meaning of gender, and what explains differences in behavior between the sexes?

3. How do preschoolers play, and how does play contribute to and reflect development?

4. How do parenting practices influence development?

5. Why do young children help or hurt others, and why do they develop fears?

6. How do young children get along with (or without) siblings, playmates, and friends?

Detailed Chapter Outline with Key Terms

I. THE DEVELOPING SELF
   A. The Self-Concept and Cognitive Development
   - **Self-concept**: Sense of self; descriptive and evaluative mental picture of one's abilities and traits.
   - *Cognitive construction:* A system of descriptive and evaluative representations about the self.
   1. Changes in Self-Definition: The 5 to 7 Shift
   - **Self-definition**: Cluster of characteristics used to describe oneself.
   - **Single representations**: In neo-Piagetian terminology, first stage in development of self-definition, in which children describe themselves in terms of individual, unconnected characteristics and in all-or-nothing terms.
   - **Real self**: The self one actually is.
   - **Ideal self**: The self one would like to be.
   - **Representational mappings**: Stage in which a child makes logical connections between one aspect of himself and another.
   - *Representational systems:* Integration of specific features of the self into a general, multidimensional concept.
   2. Cultural Differences in Self Description
   - *Interdependent* aspects of self: compliance, appropriate conduct, humility, and sense of belonging to the community.
   - *Independent* aspects of self: individuality, self-expression, and self-esteem.
   B. **Self-esteem**: The judgment a person makes about his or her self-worth.

1. Developmental Changes in Self-Esteem
2. Contingent Self-Esteem: The "Helpless" Pattern
C. Understanding and Regulating Emotions
1. Understanding Conflicting Emotions
2. Emotions Directed Toward the Self
D. Erikson: Initiative versus Guilt
- **Initiative versus guilt**: Erikson's third crisis in psychosocial development, in which children balance the urge to pursue goals with moral reservations that may prevent carrying them out.
- Purpose: The virtue that develops during this crisis and motivates a child to pursue goals without being unduly inhibited by guilt or fear of punishment.

II. GENDER
Gender identity: Awareness about ones' femaleness or maleness
A. Gender differences: Psychological or behavioral differences between males and females.
- *Gender differences:* Psychological or behavioral differences between males and females.
- *Gender similarities hypothesis:* Most gender differences are small to negligible and change with age.
B. Perspectives on Gender Development
- **Gender roles**: Behaviors, interests, attitudes, skills, and traits that a culture considers appropriate for males or females.
- **Gender-typing**: Acquisition of gender roles.
- **Gender stereotypes**: Overgeneralizations about male and female behavior.
1. *Biological Approach*: Perspective on gender development that looks at the biological bases of gender.
- *Corpus callosum:* The band of tissue joining the right and left cortical hemispheres.
- *Congenital adrenal hyperplasia (CAH:* girls with high levels of prenatal androgens, resulting in ambiguous genitalia.
2. *Evolutionary Developmental Approach*
- **Theory of Sexual Selection:** selectin of sexual partners in response to reproductive pressure for survival of the species.
3. *Psychoanalytic Approach*: Perspective on gender development that looks at gender from a Freudian viewpoint.
Identification: In Freudian theory, the process by which a young child adopts the characteristics, beliefs, attitudes, values, and behaviors of the same-sex parent.
4. *Social Learning Approach*
5. *Cognitive Approaches*: Perspective on gender development that focuses on thought processes and active construction of gender concepts.
a. Kohlberg's Cognitive-Developmental Theory
- **Gender constancy**: Awareness that one will always be male or female. Also called *sex-category constancy.*
- *Gender identity:* First stage in development of gender constancy at age 2 to 3.
- *Gender stability:* Second stage in development of gender constancy.
- *Gender consistency:* Third stage in the development of gender constancy that occurs between ages 3 and 7.

      b. **Gender-schema theory**: Theory, proposed by Bem, that children socialize themselves in their gender roles by developing a mentally organized network of information about what it means to be male or female in a particular culture.
- *Schema:* A mentally organized network of information that influences a particular category of behavior.

    6. *Socialization-Based Approach*: Perspective on gender development that emphasizes the influence of socialization and observational learning on forming gender concepts.
- **Social cognitive theory**: Albert Bandura's expansion of social learning theory; holds that children learn gender roles through socialization.
      a.   Family Influences
      b.   Peer Influences
      c.   Cultural Influences

III. PLAY: THE BUSINESS OF EARLY CHILDHOOD
- *Rough-and-tumble play:* Play that involves wrestling, kicking, and chasing.
- *Cognitive Complexity:* Cognitive involvement of play.
- *Social dimension:* Whether children play alone or with others.

  A. Cognitive Levels of Play
- **Functional play**: The lowest cognitive level of play, involving repetitive muscular movements.
- **Constructive play**: The second cognitive level of play, involving use of objects or materials to make something.
- **Dramatic play**: The third cognitive level of play, involving imaginary people or situations; also called *fantasy play, dramatic play*, or *imaginative play*.
- *Formal games with rules:* The fourth cognitive level of play, involving organized games with known procedures and penalties, such as hopscotch and marbles.

  B. The Social Dimension of Play
- Parten's types of play
- *Reticent play:* A combination of onlooker and unoccupied play categories that is associated with shyness.

  C. How Gender Influences Play
  D. How Culture Influences Play

IV. PARENTING
  A. Forms of Discipline

Discipline: Methods of molding children's character and of teaching them to exercise self-control and engage in acceptable behavior.

1. Reinforcement and Punishment
- *External reinforcements:* Rewards for behavior that come from outside the child, such as candy or praise.
- *Internal reward:* A sense of pleasure or accomplishment.
- **Corporal punishment**: Use of physical force with the intention of causing pain, but not injury, to correct or control behavior.

2. Power Assertion, Induction, and Withdrawal of Love
- **Power assertion:** Disciplinary technique intended to discourage undesirable behavior through physical or verbal enforcement of parental control.

- **Psychological Aggression:** verbal attacks that result in psychological harm such as yelling, threatening, swearing, and name calling.
  3. Inductive Reasoning, Power Assertion, and Withdrawal of Love
  - **Inductive techniques:** Disciplinary methods designed to induce desirable behavior by appealing to a child's sense of reason and fairness.
  - **Power Assertion:** Disciplinary method intended to stop undesirable behavior through physical or verbal enforcement of parental control.
  - **Withdrawal of love**: Disciplinary strategy that may involve ignoring, isolating, or showing dislike for a child.
  B. Parenting Styles
  1. Diana Baumrind and the Effectiveness of Authoritative Parenting
    - **Authoritarian**: Parenting style emphasizing control and obedience.
    - **Permissive**: Parenting style emphasizing self-expression and self-regulation.
    - **Authoritative**: Parenting style blending respect for a child's individuality with an effort to instill social values.
    - *Neglectful or uninvolved:* Parenting style in which parents focus on their own needs rather than those of the child, sometimes because of stress or depression.
  2. Support and Criticisms of Baumrind's Model
  3. Cultural Differences in Parenting Styles
  C. Special Behavioral Concerns
  1. Prosocial Behavior
    - **Altruism:** Behavior intended to help others out of inner concern and without expectation of external reward; may involve self-denial or self-sacrifice.
    - **Prosocial behavior**: Any voluntary behavior intended to help others.
  2. Aggression
    - **Instrumental aggression**: Aggressive behavior used as an instrument to achieve a goal.
    - **Hostile Aggression:** Aggressive behavior intended to hurt another person.
      a. Gender Differences in Aggression
    - **Overt aggression**: Aggression that is openly directed at its target.
    - **Relational or Social aggression**: Aggression aimed at damaging or interfering with another person's relationships, reputation, or psychological well-being; also called *covert, indirect,* or *psychological aggression.*
      b. Influences on Aggression
      c. Culture and Aggression
  3. Fearfulness

V. RELATIONSHIPS WITH OTHER CHILDREN
  A. Sibling Relationships
  B. The Only Child
  C. Playmates and Friends

True/False Self-Test

Place a T or an F in the appropriate space. These questions are taken from the chapter content, tables, key terms, Guideposts for Study, and Checkpoints.

1. ____ Children incorporate into their self-image their growing understanding of how others see them.

2. ____ Emotions such as shame and pride develop in middle childhood, not early childhood.

3. ____ Self-esteem in early childhood is primarily based upon the response of peers and teachers.

4. ____ Children who have developed representational systems can integrate their sets of positive and negative emotions.

5. ____ Older children can describe conflicting feelings toward the same target, whereas younger children cannot.

6. ____ According to Erikson, the conflict in early childhood is trust versus mistrust.

7. ____ The main gender difference in early childhood is girls' greater aggressiveness.

8. ____ Gender stereotypes peak during the preschool years.

9. ____ Gender differences are exclusively behaviorally based.

10. ____ According to Parten, play becomes less social during early childhood.

11. ____ Nonsocial play is not necessarily immature; it depends on what children do when they play.

12. ____ Discipline can be a powerful tool for socialization.

13. ____ Authoritative parents tend to raise less competent children.

14. ____ Power assertion, inductive techniques, and withdrawal of love can be effective in certain situations.

15. ____ Most children become more aggressive after age 6 or 7.

16. ____ Family conflict can be used to help children learn rules and standards of behavior and negotiating skills.

17. ____ Boys tend to practice relational aggression and girls engage in overt aggression.

18. ___ Preschool children show temporary fears of real and imagined objects.

19. ___ The psychoanalytic perspective of gender development focuses upon the process of identification.

20. ___ Most sibling interactions are negative.

21. ___ Siblings tend to resolve disputes on the basis of moral principles, although not always the same ones parents use.

22. ___ Same-sex siblings, especially girls, tend to get along better than mixed-sex siblings.

23. ___ Friends have more positive interactions and more negative interactions than do other playmates.

24. ___ Parenting does not affect children's social competence with peers.

Multiple-Choice Self-Test

Circle the letter of the best answer. These questions are based on many aspects of the chapter content, in no particular order.

1. The self-concept undergoes major change during:
a. early childhood.
b. middle childhood.
c. late childhood.
d. fourth grade.

2. According to neo-Piagetians, self-definition:
a. never changes.
b. changes unpredictably.
c. shifts from single representations to representational mappings.
d. changes according to gender only.

3. Self-esteem in early childhood tends to be:
a. unpredictable.
b. dependent on school popularity.
c. global and unrealistic.
d. conservative and realistic.

4. According to Erikson, the chief developmental crisis of early childhood is:
a. hopelessness vs. despair.
b. integrity vs. popularity.
c. initiative vs. guilt.
d. freedom vs. control.

5. The main gender difference in early childhood is:
a. girls' greater aggressiveness.
b. boys' greater aggressiveness.
c. girls' greater cognitive ability.
d. boys' greater athletic ability.

6. Gender stereotypes:
a. decline in the preschool years.
b. are unchanged until adolescence.
c. decline until adolescence.
d. peak during the preschool years.

7. The idea that gender differences are biologically based is suggested by:
a. Freud.
b. Vygotsky.
c. Erikson.
d. differences in brain size and hormonal activity.

8. According to social cognitive theory, children learn gender roles through:
a. parental instruction.
b. instinct.
c. socialization.
d. None of these.

9. According to Piaget and Smilansky, the order of cognitive progression in children's play is:
a. pretend, cognitive, functional, formal games with rules
b. cognitive, pretend, functional, formal games with rules
c. formal, functional, pretend, cognitive, constructive
d. functional, constructive, pretend, formal games with rules

10. In early childhood, children prefer to play:
a. with others of the opposite sex.
b. with others of the same sex.
c. with others of both sexes.
d. alone.

11. The most effective method of discipline is:
a. power assertion.
b. withdrawal of love.
c. inductive techniques.
d. spanking.

12. Baumrind identified:
a. three parenting styles.
b. five levels of emotional development.
c. four methods of discipline.
d. four stages of moral leadership.

13. The most common type of aggression in early childhood is:
a. overt aggression.
b. relational aggression.
c. hostile aggression.
d. instrumental aggression.

14. Relational aggression includes:
a. teasing.
b. spreading rumors.
c. exclusion from groups.
d. All of these.

15. Sibling and peer relationships contribute to:
a. self-efficacy.
b. aggression.
c. the helpless syndrome.
d. shyness.

16. Most sibling interactions are:
a. negative.
b. altruistic.
c. positive.
d. undefined.

17. Only children seem to develop:
a. social skills more slowly than children with siblings.
b. as well as children with siblings.
c. with unusual grace.
d. behind children with siblings, academically speaking.

18. Preschoolers choose playmates and friends who are:
a. unlike them.
b. like them.
c. leaders.
d. None of these.

19. Aggressive children of preschool age are:
a. more popular than prosocial children.
b. less popular than prosocial children.
c. a disappointment to their parents.
d. None of these.

20. The cluster of characteristics used to describe oneself is known as:
a. self-concept.
b. self-definition.
c. real self.
d. ideal self.

21. When a child adopts the characteristics, beliefs, attitudes, values, and behavior of the same-sex parent, it is known as:
a. gender constancy.
b. gender stereotype.
c. identification.
d. gender schema.

22. Play involving use of objects or materials to make something is classified as:
a. pretend play.
b. functional play.
c. dramatic play.
d. constructive play.

23. A discipline strategy designed to discourage undesirable behavior through physical or verbal enforcement of parental control is known as:
a. permissive.
b. power assertion.
c. altruism.
d. instrumental aggression.

24. After age 6 or 7, children become:
a. less aggressive.
b. more aggressive.
c. more inclined to pout.
d. more likely to have temper tantrums.

25. According to Kohlberg, gender constancy leads to:
a. frustration.
b. acquisition of gender roles.
c. preadolescence.
d. cognitive competence.

Short Essay Questions

These short essay questions are based on the Checkpoints in the chapter. Answer each question as completely and succinctly as possible. Check your answers by reviewing the part of the chapter that covers the Guidepost listed with each question.

1. Describe the emergence of altruism and the ways it is influenced in early childhood. (See Guidepost 5.)

2. Describe the benefits of the sibling relationship and the ways sibling interactions help children to develop. (See Guidepost 6).

3. Explain why Baumrind's categories of parenting styles may not be appropriate for all cultures. (See Guidepost 4.)

4. Discuss the ways in which children become aware of gender in early childhood. (See Guidepost 2.)

Organize It!

Here are several helpful lists to make. Practice memorizing the lists and you will find that the chapter information is organized in a meaningful whole in your mind!

1. List and briefly describe the six major theoretical perspectives on gender development. (See Guidepost 2.)

    1.

    2.

    3.

    4.

    5.

    6.

2. List and describe the four parenting styles described by Baumrind, Maccoby, and Martin. (See Guidepost 4.)

    1.

    2.

    3.

    4.

3. List and describe the common fears of childhood, including the ages when they most commonly appear. (See Table 8-3 and Guidepost 5.)

    1.

    2.

    3.

    4.

    5.

    6.

    7.

    8.

    9.

    10.

4. List and describe four cognitive levels of play, according to Piaget and others. (See Guidepost 3.)

    1.

    2.

    3.

    4.

5. List Parten's six categories of social and nonsocial play. (See Guidepost 3).

    1.

    2.

    3.

    4.

    5.

    6.

6. List and give examples of the five different types of psychological aggression.

    1.

    2.

    3.

    4.

    5.

Critical Thinking Questions

These questions may be used in small group discussions or as extra-credit reports. (Remember that extra-credit reports are only available if your instructor agrees.)

1. What are some ways in which your parents or other adults helped you develop self-esteem?

2. Should parents encourage their children to play with toys that are typically for the other gender, such as boys playing with dolls and girls playing with trucks? How might parents discourage sex-role stereotypes?

3. Have computers and calculators been good for children's cognitive development? Why or why not?

4. In what situations is spanking a child acceptable?

5. What kind of parent do you think you are or will be, according to Baumrind's categories? What kind of parenting style did your own parents use?

6. Are there situations in which a child should be encouraged to be aggressive?

7. What kind of problems do you foresee if the United States adopted a "one child" policy as in China?

Answer Keys

True/False Self-Test

1.	T	GP 1		13. F	GP 4
2.	F	GP 1		14. T	GP 4
3.	F	GP 1		15. F	GP 5
4.	T	GP 1		16. T	GP 5
5.	T	GP 1		17. F	GP 5
6.	F	GP 1		18. T	GP 5
7.	F	GP 2		19. T	GP 2
8.	T	GP 2		20. F	GP 6
9.	F	GP 2		21. T	GP 6
10.	F	GP 3		22. T	GP 6
11.	T	GP 3		23. T	GP 6
12.	T	GP 4		24. F	GP 6

Multiple-Choice Self-Test

1.	a	GP 1		14. d	GP 5
2.	c	GP 1		15. a	GP 6
3.	c	GP 1		16. c	GP 6
4.	c	GP 1		17. b	GP 6
5.	b	GP 2		18. b	GP 6
6.	d	GP 2		19. b	GP 5
7.	d	GP 2		20. b	GP 1
8.	c	GP 2		21. c	GP 2
9.	d	GP 3		22. d	GP 3
10.	b	GP 3		23. b	GP 4
11.	c	GP 4		24. a	GP 5
12.	a	GP 4		25 b	GP 2
13.	d	GP 5			

PART 4: MIDDLE CHILDHOOD

CHAPTER 9: PHYSICAL AND COGNITIVE DEVELOPMENT IN MIDDLE CHILDHOOD

Chapters 9 and 10 make up Part 4 of the text, which explores middle childhood. The middle years from 6 to 11 are often termed the *school years*. School is a focal point of physical, cognitive, and psychosocial development. Children grow taller, heavier, and stronger, and they acquire the motor skills needed to participate in organized games and sports. This chapter focuses on physical and cognitive skills.

Guideposts for Study

1. What gains in growth and motor development occur in school-age children, and what are their nutritional needs?

2. What are the principal health and fitness concerns for school-age children, and what can be done to make these years healthier and safer?

3. How do school-age children's thinking and moral reasoning differ from those of younger children?

4. What advances in memory and other information-processing skills occur during middle childhood?

5. How accurately can schoolchildren's' intelligence be measured?

6. How do communicative abilities and literacy expand during middle childhood?

7. How do children adjust to school, and what influences school achievement?

8. How do schools meet special needs?

Detailed Chapter Outline with Key Terms

PHYSICAL DEVELOPMENT
I. Aspects of Physical Development
   A. Height and Weight
   B. Nutrition and Sleep
   C. Brain Development
      • *Loss in density of gray matter*
      • *Increase in white matter*
   C. Motor Development and Physical Play
     1. Recess-Time Play
      • **Rough-and-Tumble Play**: Vigorous play involving wrestling, hitting, and chasing, often accompanied by laughing and screaming.
     2. Organized Sports
II. HEALTH, FITNESS, AND SAFETY

A. Obesity and Body Image
- Body Image: How one believes one looks.
1. Causes of Obesity
2. Why is Childhood Obesity a Serious Concern?
3. Prevention and Treatment
B. Other Medical Problems
- **Acute medical condition:** occasional, short-term condition, such as allergies or a cold
- **Chronic medical condition:** physical, developmental, behavioral, or emotional condition requiring special health services
1. Stuttering: involuntary audible or silent repetition or prolongation of sounds or syllables
2. Asthma
- **Asthma**: A chronic respiratory disease characterized by sudden attacks of coughing, wheezing, and difficulty in breathing
C. Accidental Injuries

COGNITIVE DEVELOPMENT
III. Piagetian Approach: The Concrete Operational Child
Concrete operations: Third stage of Piagetian cognitive development (approximately from ages 7 to 12), during which children develop logical but not abstract thinking.
A. Cognitive Advances
1. Space Relationships and Causality
2. Categorization
- **Seriation**: Ability to order items along a dimension.
- **Transitive inference**: Understanding of the relationship between two objects by knowing the relationship of each to a third object.
- **Class inclusion**: Understanding the relationship between a whole and its parts.
3. Inductive and Deductive Reasoning
- **Inductive reasoning**: Type of logical reasoning that moves from particular observations about members of a class to a general conclusion about that class.
- **Deductive reasoning**: Type of logical reasoning that moves from a general premise about a class to a conclusion about a particular member(s) of the class.
4. Conservation
- *Identity:* Knowledge that a substance retains its nature even when it looks different.
- *Reversibility:* Knowledge that reversing an action will cause the substance to revert to its former appearance.
- *Decenter:* Ability to focus on more than one feature of a stimulus at a time.
5. Number and Mathematics
B. Influences of Neurological Development, Culture, and Schooling
C. Moral Reasoning
Equity: The belief that one person may be treated differently than another because of special circumstances that are taken into account.

- Rigid obedience to authority: first stage of moral reasoning that does not consider intent.
- Increasing flexibility: second state of moral reasoning that does consider intent.

IV. Information Processing Approach: Planning, Attention, and Memory
- **Executive Function:** the conscious control of thoughts, emotions, and actions to accomplish goals and solve problems.
  A. How Do Executive Skills Develop?
  B. Selective Attention
     - Selective Attention: The ability to deliberately direct one's attention and shut out distractions.
     - Inhibitory Control: The voluntary suppression of unwanted responses.
  C. Working Memory Span
  D. Metamemory: Understanding Memory
     - *Metamemory*: Knowledge about the processes of memory.
  E. Mnemonics: Strategies for Remembering
     - **Mnemonic strategies:** Devices to aid memory.
     - **External memory aids**: Mnemonic strategies using something outside the person.
     - **Rehearsal**: Mnemonic strategy to keep an item in working memory through conscious repetition.
     - **Organization**: Mnemonic strategy of categorizing material to be remembered.
     - **Elaboration**: Mnemonic strategy of making mental associations involving items to be remembered.
  F. Information Processing and Piagetian Tasks

V. PSYCHOMETRIC APPROACH: ASSESSMENT OF INTELLIGENCE
- **Wechsler Intelligence Scale for Children (WISC-III)**: Individual intelligence test for schoolchildren, which yields verbal and performance scores as well as a combined score.
- **Otis-Lennon School Ability Test**: Group intelligence test for kindergarten through 12th grade.
  A. The IQ Controversy
     1. Influence of Schooling
     2. Influences on Intelligence
     a. Influences of Brain Development
     b. Influence of Schooling
     c. Influences of Race/Ethnicity and Socioeconomic Status
     d. Influence of Culture
        - **Cultural bias**: Tendency of intelligence tests to include items calling for knowledge or skills that are more familiar or meaningful to some cultural groups than to others.
        - **Culture-free**: Describing an intelligence test that, if it were possible to design, would have no culturally linked content.
        - **Culture-fair**: Describing an intelligence test that deals with experiences common to various cultures, in an attempt to avoid cultural bias.
        - *Successful Intelligence:* Skills and knowledge needed for success within a particular social and cultural context.

- **Culture-relevant Tests:** Tests that take into account the adaptive taks that confront children in particular cultures.
  - B. Is There More Than One Intelligence?
    1. Gardner's Theory of Multiple intelligences
       - o **Theory of Multiple Intelligences:** View that intelligence includes linguistic, logical-mathematical, spatial, musical, bodily-kinesthetic, interpersonal, and intrapersonal.
    2. Sternberg's **Triarchic Theory of Intelligence**: Three types of intelligence: componential, experiential, and contextual.
       - **Componential element**: The analytic aspect of intelligence. *Analytic:* The ability to process information efficiently, as in problem-solving.
       - **Experiential element**: The insightful aspect of intelligence. *Insightful:* In Sternberg's theory, the ability to think originally and creatively.
       - **Contextual element**: The practical aspect of intelligence. *Practical:* The ability to size up a situation and decide what to do: adapt to it, change it, or get out of it.
       - **Tacit knowledge**: Practical knowledge that is not explicitly taught but is gained informally.
       - *The Sternberg Triarchic Abilities Test (STAT)*: Test that seeks to measure each of the three components of intelligence through multiple-choice and essay questions in three domains: verbal, quantitative, and figural (or spatial).
  - C. Other Directions in Intelligence Testing
    - **Kaufman Assessment Battery for Children (K-ABC)**: Nontraditional individual intelligence test designed to provide fair assessments of minority children and children with disabilities.
    - *Dynamic testing:* Testing of intelligence based on Vygotsky's theory of cognitive development and the zone of proximal development.
- VI. LANGUAGE
  - A. Vocabulary, Grammar, and Syntax
    - *Simile* and *metaphor:* Figures of speech in which a word or phrase that usually designates one thing is compared or applied to another.
    - *Syntax:* How words are organized into phrases and sentences.
  - B. Pragmatics: Knowledge about Communications
    - *Pragmatics:* The practical use of language to communicate.
  - C. Second-language Learning
    - **English-immersion**: children are immersed in English from the beginning in special classes.
    - **Bilingual education**: children are taught in two languages, first learning in their native language and then switching to regular classes.
    - **Bilingual**: fluent in two languages
    - **Two way or dual language learning**: English and non-English speaking children learn together and use each other's languages.
- VII. THE CHILD IN SCHOOL
  - A. Entering First Grade
    1. Becoming literate

- **Decoding**: Process by which a child sounds out a word, translating it from print to speech before retrieving it from long-term memory.
- **Visually based retrieval**: Process by which a child simply looks at a word and then retrieves it.
- **Phonetic, or code emphasis approach**: Approach to teaching reading that emphasizes decoding of unfamiliar words.
- **Whole-language approach**: Approach to teaching reading that emphasizes visual retrieval and use of contextual cues.
- **Metacognition**: Awareness of one's own thinking processes.

B. Influences on School Achievement
  1. Self-Efficacy Beliefs and Academic Motivation
     Self-efficacy: Belief that one's actions will bring about a particular result, either favorable or unfavorable.
  2. Gender
  3. Parenting Practices
     - *Authoritative:* Parenting style blending respect for a child's individuality with an effort to instill social values.
     - *Authoritarian:* Parenting style emphasizing control and obedience.
     - *Permissive:* Parenting style emphasizing self-expression and self-regulation.
  4. Socioeconomic Status
     Social capital: Family and community resources on which a child can draw.
  5. Peer Acceptance
  5. Educational Methods
  6. Class size
  7. Educational Innovations
     - Social promotion: Policy of automatically promoting children even if they do not meet academic standards.

VIII. Educating Children with Special Needs
A. Children with Learning Problems
  1. **Mental Retardation**: Significantly subnormal cognitive functioning.
  2. Learning Disabilities
     - **Dyslexia**: Developmental disorder in which reading achievement is substantially lower than predicted by IQ or age.
     - **Learning disabilities (LDs)**: Disorders that interfere with specific aspects of learning and school achievement.
  3. Attention-Deficit/Hyperactivity Disorder
     - **Attention-deficit/hyperactivity disorder (ADHD)**: Syndrome characterized by persistent inattention and distractibility, impulsivity, low tolerance for frustration, and inappropriate overactivity.
  4. Educating Children with Disabilities
B. Gifted Children
  1. What is Special about Gifted Children?
  2. Defining and Measuring Creativity
     - **Creativity**: Ability to see situations in a new way, to produce innovations, or to discern previously unidentified problems and find novel solutions.
     - **Convergent thinking**: Thinking aimed at finding the "one" right answer to a

problem.
- **Divergent thinking**: Thinking that produces a variety of fresh, diverse possibilities.
3. Educating Gifted Children
   - **Enrichment**: Approach to educating the gifted, which broadens and deepens knowledge and skills through extra activities, projects, field trips, or mentoring.
   - **Acceleration**: Approach to educating the gifted, which moves them through the curriculum at an unusually rapid pace.

True/False Self-Test

Place a T or an F in the appropriate space. These questions are taken from the chapter content, tables, key terms, Guideposts for Study, and Checkpoints.

1. _____ Physical development is more rapid in middle childhood than in early childhood.

2. _____ On the average, children need 5,000 calories per day to maintain growth and development.

3. _____ In the United States, one child in five does not get enough to eat.

4. _____ Concern with body image increases in middle childhood.

5. _____ Malnutrition can affect cognitive and psychosocial development.

6. _____ Obesity is increasingly rare among U.S. children.

7. _____ Lack of exercise affects mental health.

8. _____ About 89% of schoolchildren's free play is rough-and-tumble play.

9. _____ Teaching non-English-speaking children in English only is the most effective method of education.

10. _____ Vision becomes keener in middle childhood.

11. _____ Chronic medical conditions, such as asthma, are more common among upper-class children.

12. _____ Children's understanding of health and illness is related to their cognitive level.

13. _____ Phonics is a much better method of teaching reading than visual retrieval or the whole language method.

14. _____ Children are less proficient at tasks involving conservation, spatial thinking, transitive inference, and inductive reasoning in middle childhood than they are in early childhood.

15. ____ Cultural experience seems to contribute to the rate of development of conservation and other Piagetian skills.

16. ____ According to Piaget, the first stage of moral reasoning in middle childhood is the morality of obedience.

17. ____ Information-processing theory looks at eight stages of memory.

18. ____ The capacity of working memory increases greatly during middle childhood.

19. ____ Metamemory disappears in middle childhood.

20. ____ Rehearsal, organization, and elaboration are all mnemonic strategies.

21. ____ The WISC-III and the Stanford-Binet IQ tests are both group tests.

22. ____ Conventional IQ tests may miss important aspects of intelligent behavior.

23. ____ According to Robert Sternberg's triarchic theory of intelligence, IQ tests measure mainly the componential element of intelligence, not the experiential or contextual elements.

24. ____ Schooling seems to increase measured intelligence.

25. ____ Studies on bilingualism have shown that being bilingual lowers a child's cognitive achievement.

Multiple-Choice Self-Test

Circle the letter of the best answer. These questions are based on many aspects of the chapter content, in no particular order.

1. Which of the following is true about mental retardation?
a. It most often appears after age 18.
b. It is indicated by an IQ of about 70 or less.
c. It occurs in 20% of the U.S. population.
d. Mental retardation is the same as dyslexia.

2. Creativity and IQ are:
a. closely linked.
b. likely to go together.
c. not closely linked.
d. the same thing.

3. In Terman's study, most of the children were:
a. millionaires in adulthood.
b. well-adjusted and successful.
c. below average in IQ.
d. mildly retarded.

4. Tests of creativity attempt to measure:
a. divergent thinking.
b. convergent thinking.
c. sensory memory.
d. working memory.

5. Programs for gifted children are often based on:
a. enrichment.
b. acceleration.
c. Both acceleration and enrichment..
d. None of these.

6. A common standard for identifying gifted children for special programs is an IQ of:
a. 130 or higher.
b. 200 or higher.
c. 65 or higher.
d. 44 or higher.

7. An understanding of the relationship between two objects by knowing the relationship of each to a third object is:
a. class inclusion.
b. seriation.
c. transitive inference.
d. inductive reasoning.

8. The ability to order items along a dimension is:
a. inductive reasoning.
b. seriation.
c. class inclusion.
d. cross-modal transfer.

9. In Piaget's terminology, the inconsistency in development in different types of conservation is called:
a. encoding.
b. morality of constraint.
c. morality of cooperation.
d. horizontal décalage.

10. A strategy to improve memory by using a variety of devices is called:
a. metamemory.
b. cognitive development.
c. mnemonics.
d. retrieval.

11. Understanding the processes of memory is:
a. central executive.
b. storage.
c. metamemory.
d. encoding.

12. A type of logical reasoning that moves from a general premise about a class to a conclusion about a particular member or members of the class is:
a. deductive reasoning.
b. inductive reasoning.
c. metacognition.
d. horizontal décalage.

13. A developmental disorder in which reading achievement is substantially lower than predicted by IQ or age is:
a. ADD.
b. ODD.
c. dyslexia.
d. autism.

14. A set of linguistic rules that govern the use of language for communication is:
a. metacognition.
b. pragmatics.
c. child-directed speech.
d. bilingualism.

15. Thinking that is aimed at finding the "one right answer" to a problem is:
a. divergent thinking.
b. convergent thinking.
c. enrichment.
d. acceleration of ideas.

16. The most commonly diagnosed learning disability is:
a. ADHD.
b. dyslexia.
c. mental retardation.
d. autism.

17. The superior achievement of children of East Asian extraction seems to stem from:
a. cultural factors.
b. homework assigned.
c. parental discipline.
d. higher IQ.

18. The major area of linguistic growth in middle childhood is in:
a. vocabulary.
b. grammar.
c. syntax.
d. pragmatics.

19. According to Piaget, the development of moral reasoning:
a. is linked with cognitive maturation.
b. occurs in two stages.
c. Both of these.
d. Neither of these.

20. In order to reduce injuries and fatalities for school-age children, parents should:
a. keep their children inside as much as possible.
b. encourage the use of bicycle helmets.
c. encourage children to sit still and watch television.
d. forbid them to ride bicycles.

21. Children in the stage of concrete operations are:
a. largely limited to the present in their reasoning.
b. less egocentric than before.
c. more proficient at logical reasoning tasks.
d. All of these.

22. Rough-and-tumble play is:
a. more common among boys than girls.
b. more common among girls than boys.
c. the way children spend 90% of their free-play time.
d. known to increase after age 11.

23. On the average, how many calories per day do children need to maintain growth and development?
a. 3,600
b. 2,400
c. 4,500
d. 6,500

24. African American children grow:
a. faster than white children.
b. slower than white children.
c. at the same rate as white children.
d. less muscle and less bone mass than white children.

25. Obesity is:
a. decreasing among U.S. children.
b. influenced by genetics and environmental factors.
c. less common in U.S. children than in Japanese children.
d. a result of parental neglect.

Short Essay Questions

These short essay questions are based on the Checkpoints in the chapter. Answer each question as completely and succinctly as possible. Check your answers by reviewing the part of the chapter that covers the Guidepost listed with each question.

1. On the basis of the descriptions in the chapter, which approach to second-language education do you favor? Support your position with research. (See Guidepost 6.)

2. Is intelligence related to how well a person adapts to the dominant culture, or should intelligence tests be designed to take a minority culture into account (see Guidepost 5)?

3. According to Piaget's theory of moral development, more mature moral judgments consider intent, not just the seriousness of the offense. Do you agree that intent is an important factor in morality? In what ways does the criminal justice system reflect this view? (See Guidepost 3.)

4. Based on what you have read in your textbook, what can you say about the importance of maintaining physical fitness in school-aged children? What suggestions can you make for motivating all children to stay physically fit? (See Guidepost 1.)

5. In view of childhood malnutrition's long-term effects on physical, social, and cognitive development, what can and should various sectors of society—government agencies, community groups, and private organizations—do to combat it? (See Guidepost 1.)

Organize It!

Making lists is a fun and useful way to categorize information in your mind. After making each list, think of ways to memorize it so that you have immediate recall. Singing a list, dancing while you recite it, or simply saying it in a rhythmic pattern as you are walking, driving, or jogging allows your brain to store the information in easily retrievable form. Try it!

1. List the three principles that help school-aged children understand conservation. (See Guidepost 3.)

    1.

    2.

    3.

2. List and describe Piaget's three stages of moral development. (See Guidepost 3.)

    1.

    2.

    3.

3. List and briefly describe Howard Gardner's eight intelligences. (See Guidepost 5.)

    1.

    2.

    3.

4.

5.

6.

7.

8.

4. List and describe two intelligence tests for schoolchildren. (See Guidepost 5.)

    1.

    2.

5. List four of the most common mnemonic aids. (See Guidepost 4.)

    1.

    2.

    3.

    4.

6. List and briefly describe Sternberg's three components of intelligence. (See Guidepost 5.)

    1.

    2.

    3.

Critical Thinking Questions

These questions may be used in small group discussions or as extra-credit reports (if your instructor agrees with extra credit).

1. Should the government force parents to make their children wear helmets when riding bicycles, scooters, and skateboards?

2. On which of Piaget's two levels of moral development does our criminal justice system work? Support your answer with examples.

3. Should IQ test scores be used to determine who gets into programs for special education and gifted education? Why or why not? What would some alternative assessment techniques be?

4. What is a reasonable amount of homework for one evening for a child in elementary school? For 1 week? What about a middle-school student?

5. Should stimulants be used to treat ADHD? Who should diagnosis a child with ADHD?

6. Should gifted children get special educational attention? Why or why not?

Answer Keys

True/False Self-Test

1.	F	GP 1	14.	F	GP 3
2.	F	GP 1	15.	T	GP 3
3.	T	GP 1	16.	T	GP 3
4.	T	GP 2	17.	F	GP 4
5.	T	GP 1	18.	T	GP 4
6.	F	GP 2	19.	F	GP 4
7.	T	GP 2	20.	T	GP 4
8.	F	GP 2	21.	F	GP 5
9.	F	GP 8	22.	T	GP 5
10.	T	GP 2	23.	T	GP 5
11.	F	GP 2	24.	T	GP 7
12.	T	GP 2	25.	F	GP 8
13.	F	GP 7			

Multiple-Choice Self-Test

1.	b	GP 8	14.	b	GP 6
2.	c	GP 8	15.	b	GP 8
3.	b	GP 8	16.	b	GP 8
4.	a	GP 8	17.	a	GP 7
5.	c	GP 8	18.	d	GP 6
6.	a	GP 8	19.	a	GP 3
7.	c	GP 3	20.	b	GP 2
8.	b	GP 3	21.	d	GP 3
9.	d	GP 3	22.	a	GP 2
10.	c	GP 4	23.	b	GP 1
11.	c	GP 4	24.	a	GP 1
12.	a	GP 3	25.	b	GP 2
13.	c	GP 8			

CHAPTER 10: PSYCHOSOCIAL DEVELOPMENT IN MIDDLE CHILDHOOD

This chapter introduces school-age children in the context of self-esteem, emotional growth, family atmosphere and structure, peer group friendships, and mental health.

Guideposts for Study

1. How do school-age children develop a realistic self-concept, and how do they show emotional growth?

2. How do parent-child relationships change in middle childhood, and how do family atmosphere and structure influence children's well-being?

3. How do relationships with peers change in middle childhood, and what influences popularity and choice of friends?

4. What are the most common forms of aggressive behavior in middle childhood, and what influences contribute to it?

5. What are some common emotional disturbances, and how are they treated?

6. How do the stresses of modern life affect children, and what enables "resilient" children to withstand them?

Detailed Chapter Outline with Key Terms

I. THE DEVELOPING SELF
   A. Self-concept Development: Representational Systems
      - **Representational systems**: The third stage in development of self-definition, characterized by breadth, balance, and integration and assessment of various aspects of the self.
      - *Real self:* Your knowledge of who you really are.
      - *Ideal self:* Knowledge of who you would like to be or think you should be.
      - *Global self-worth:* value of self as a person.
   B. Self-Esteem
      - **Industry versus inferiority**: Erikson's fourth stage of psychosocial development, in which children must learn the productive skills their culture requires or else face feelings of inferiority.
      - *Competence:* The "virtue" that develops in Erikson's fourth stage, a view of the self as able to master skills and complete tasks.
   C. Emotional Growth and Prosocial Behavior
II. THE CHILD IN THE FAMILY
   A. Family Atmosphere
      - **Internalizing Behaviors:** anxiety, fearfulness, and depression
      - **Externalizing Behaviors:** aggression, fighting, disobedience, and hostility.

1. Parenting Issues: From Control to Coregulation
   Coregulation: Transitional stage in the control of behavior in which parents exercise general supervision and children exercise moment-to-moment self-regulation.
2. Effects of Parents' Work
   - *Self care:* Children who care for themselves at home without adult supervision.
3. Poverty and Parenting
B. Family Structure
   1. When Parents Divorce
      a. Adjusting to Divorce
      b. Custody, Visitation, and Co-parenting
      - *Joint custody:* Custody of a minor child shared by both parents.
         o *Legal:* Type of joint custody in which parents share the right and responsibility to make decisions regarding the child's welfare.
         o *Physical:* Type of joint custody in which parents have the child or children live with each of them part of the time.
      c. Long-Term Effects
   2. Living in a One-Parent Family
   3. Living in a Cohabiting Family
   4. Living in a Stepfamily
   5. Living with Gay or Lesbian Parents
   6. Adoptive Families
      Open adoption: Type of adoption in which the parties share information or have direct contact.
   1. Adoptive Families
      Open adoption: Type of adoption in which the parties share information or have direct contact.
C. Sibling Relationships
III. THE CHILD IN THE PEER GROUP
   A. Positive and Negative Influences of Peer Relations
   Prejudice: Unfavorable attitude toward members of certain groups outside one's own, especially racial or ethnic groups.
   B. Popularity
      - *Sociometric popularity:* Research measure that determines which children are liked most and least by their peers.
      - *Peer Status Groups:* Five groups of children based upon popularity.
        - *Popular:* Child that receives many positive nominations from peers.
        - *Rejected:* Child that receives many negative nominations from peers.
        - *Neglected:* Child that receives few nominations of either kind.
        - *Controversial:* Child that receives many positive nominations but also receives many negative ones.
        - *Average:* Child that receives a typical number of both positive and negative nominations.
        - *Perceived popularity:* Measure of popularity that is determined by asking the child who is best liked by peers.
   C. Friendship
   D. Aggression and Bullying

- **Instrumental aggression:** Aggression aimed at achieving an objective.
- **Hostile aggression:** Aggressive behavior intended to hurt another person.
- *Overt aggression:* Physical form of aggression.
- *Relational aggression:* Social aggression, such as insulting someone or spreading rumors about that person.

1. Aggression and Social Information Processing
    - *Proactive aggression:* Another term for instrumental aggression.
    - *Reactive aggressor:* Another term for hostile aggression on the part of an individual.
    - *Hostile attribution bias, or hostile attribution of intent:* When a child sees other children as trying to hurt him or her and strikes out angrily in retaliation or self-defense.

2. Types of Aggression and Social Information Processing
3. Does Media Violence Stimulate Aggression?
3. Bullies and Victims
    - **Bullying:** Aggression deliberately and persistently directed against a particular target, or victim, typically one who is weak, vulnerable, and defenseless.

IV. MENTAL HEALTH
Mental health: The emotional health of a person.
A. Common Emotional Disorders
    - *Disruptive conduct disorders:* Disorders having to do with undesirable behavior, such as aggression or defiance, stealing, and other antisocial behavior.
    - *Anxiety disorders:* Disorders having to do with excessive fear or anxiety.
    - *Mood disorders:* Disorders having to do with emotional imbalances, such as sadness or depression.

1. Disruptive Conduct Disorders
    - **Oppositional defiant disorder (ODD):** Pattern of defiance, disobedience, and hostility toward adult authority figures lasting for at least six months and going beyond the bounds of normal childhood behavior.
    - **Conduct disorder (CD):** Persistent, repetitive pattern, beginning at an early age, of aggressive, antisocial acts, such as truancy, setting fires, habitual lying, fighting, bullying, theft, vandalism, assaults, and drug and alcohol use.

2. School Phobia and Other Anxiety Disorders
    - **School phobia:** Unrealistic fear of going to school.
    - **Separation anxiety disorder:** Condition involving excessive anxiety for at least four weeks concerning separation from home or from people to whom a child is attached.
    - **Social phobia** or Social Anxiety: Extreme fear and/or avoidance of social situations such as speaking in class or meeting an acquaintance on the street.
    - **Generalized anxiety disorder:** Anxiety not focused on any single target.
    - **Obsessive-compulsive disorder (OCD):** Anxiety aroused by repetitive, intrusive thoughts, images, or impulses, often leading to ritualistic behaviors.

3. **Childhood Depression:** disorder of mood that goes beyond normal, temporary sadness.

B. Treatment Techniques
- **Individual psychotherapy**: Psychological treatment in which a therapist sees a troubled person one-on-one.
- **Family Therapy**: The therapist sees the family together, observes how members interact, and points out both growth-producing and destructive patterns of family
- **Behavior therapy**: A form of psychotherapy using principles of learning theory to develop desired behaviors or eliminate undesired ones.
  - *Cognitive Behavioral Therapy:* Therapeutic approach which seeks to change negative thoughts through gradual exposure, modeling, rewards, or "self talk."
- **Art therapy**: Therapeutic approach that allows a child to express troubled feelings without words, using a variety of art materials and media.
- **Play therapy**: Therapeutic approach in which a child plays freely while a therapist observes and occasionally comments, asks questions, or makes suggestions.
- **Drug therapy**: Administration of drugs to treat emotional disorders.
  - *Selective serotonin reuptake inhibitors (SSRIs)*: Drugs shown to be effective in treating obsessive-compulsive, depressive, and anxiety disorders.

C. Stress and Resilience
1. Stresses of Modern Life
2. Coping with Stress: The Resilient Child
- **Resilient children**: Children who weather adverse circumstances, function well despite challenges or threats, or bounce back from traumatic events.
- **Protective factors**: Influences that reduce the impact of early stress and tend to predict positive outcomes.
  - *Family relationships:* A factor that, when positive, can be a protective influence in helping children and adolescents overcome stress.
  - *Cognitive functioning:* A factor that, when at a high level, can be a protective influence in helping children and adolescents overcome stress.
  - *The child's personality:* An adaptable, friendly, and competent personality can be a positive influence in dealing with stress.
  - *Compensating experiences:* A supportive school environment or successful experiences in areas such as studies, sports, music, or with other persons, which can help make up for a destructive home life.
  - *Reduced risk:* Exposure of the child to only one risk factor, such as poverty or mental illness, which allows a child to better overcome stress.

True/False Self-Test

Place a T or an F in the appropriate space. These questions are taken from the chapter content, tables, key terms, Guideposts for Study, and Checkpoints.

1. _____ The cognitive growth that takes place during middle childhood enables children to develop in emotional understanding and control.

2. _____ The self-concept becomes less realistic during middle childhood.

3. _____ According to Erikson, the chief source of self-esteem is children's view of their productive competence.

4. _____ School-age children have internalized shame and pride.

5. _____ School-age children spend less time with their parents, but relationships with parents continue to be important.

6. _____ Coregulation is an intermediate stage in the transfer of control from parent to child.

7. _____ Homes with employed mothers tend to be less structured and less egalitarian than homes with stay-at-home mothers.

8. _____ Boys in lower-class families tend to do less well if their mothers work.

9. _____ Parents living in poverty may not be able to provide effective discipline.

10. _____ Maternal employment has a positive influence on children's school achievement in low-income families.

11. _____ Research has shown little relationship between violence in the media and aggression.

12. _____ Open adoption strongly affects children's adjustment and parents' satisfaction.

13. _____ One of the most important effects of family structure is in its impact on family atmosphere.

14. _____ Unwed motherhood creates fewer single-parent families than does divorce.

15. _____ A child can be diagnosed with school phobia after one incident of fearing attending school.

16. _____ Girls adjust to stepfathers more readily than do boys.

17. _____ The best documented therapy for children is cognitive behavioral techniques.

18. ___ Boys adjust better than do girls to the mother's remarriage.

19. ___ Despite public concern about children living with homosexual parents, studies have found no ill effects.

20. ___ Siblings in nonindustrialized societies teach their younger siblings more than do those in industrialized societies.

21. ___ Peer groups can have negative and positive effects on a child's development.

22. ___ Siblings have less structured roles and responsibilities in nonindustrialized countries.

23. ___ Relationships with parents do not affect sibling relationships.

24. ___ The peer group becomes more important in middle childhood.

25. ___ Resilient children are less able than others to withstand the negative effects of stress.

Multiple-Choice Self-Test

Circle the letter of the best answer. These questions are based on many aspects of the chapter content, in no particular order.

1. Broad, inclusive self-concepts that integrate different aspects of the self are known as:
   a. social strata.
   b. representational systems.
   c. self-concept.
   d. None of these.

2. Harter's research suggests that
   a. the "virtue" that develops with being able to master skills and complete tasks is competence.
   b. today's U.S. school-age children judge themselves more by good looks and popularity than by skills.
   c. Neither of these.
   d. Both of these.

3. Child development is most strongly influenced by:
   a. television.
   b. the church.
   c. home atmosphere.
   d. discipline outside the home.

4. The stage in which parents and children share power is known as:
   a. adolescence.
   b. coregulation.
   c. conflict.
   d. strategic.

5. Through family conflict, children learn about:
   a. rules and standards of behavior.
   b. winning arguments.
   c. manipulation.
   d. None of these.

6. McLloyd's research suggests that which of the following is an effect of poverty on *adults*?
   a. anxiety
   b. depression
   c. decreased responsiveness to children
   d. All of these.

7. The ethnic group that has been consistently least likely to put their babies up for adoption is:
   a. Latino women.
   b. Black women.
   c. White women.
   d. Asian women.

8. A typical reaction to violence in middle childhood is:
   a. acting out and self-destructive behavior.
   b. identification with the aggressor.
   c. bed-wetting.
   d. aggressiveness.

9. According to Erikson, a major determinant of self-esteem is:
   a. children's view of their capacity for productive work.
   b. appearance.
   c. athletic ability.
   d. popularity.

10. One important aspect of emotional growth is:
    a. control of negative emotions.
    b. learning the difference between having an emotion and expressing it.
    c. learning how other people react to a display of emotions.
    d. All of these.

11. Parents who acknowledge their children's feelings of distress encourage:
a. dependency.
b. empathy and prosocial development.
c. independence.
d. suppression of emotions.

12. Shame and pride develop by age:
a. 5 or 6.
b. 7 or 8.
c. 9 or 10.
d. 10 or 11.

13. Prosocial children tend to:
a. act appropriately in social situations.
b. be relatively free from negative emotion.
c. cope with problems constructively.
d. All of these.

14. During the period of coregulation, parents rely on:
a. direct management of the child.
b. minimal contact with the child.
c. discussion with the child.
d. the school.

15. The processes by which parents and children resolve conflicts is often:
a. more important than specific outcomes.
b. full of violence.
c. less important than the outcomes.
d. full of anger.

16. As children become preadolescents:
a. discipline becomes easier.
b. the quality of family problem-solving often deteriorates.
c. they require less autonomy.
d. they become more positive in their negotiations.

17. The impact of a mother's work on school-age children depends on:
a. the child's age.
b. how she feels about her work.
c. if her mate is supportive.
d. All of these.

18. Which of the following accurately describes school-age children of employed mothers, compared to those with stay-at-home mothers?
a. They are encouraged to be more independent.
b. They live in less structured homes.
c. They have fewer household responsibilities.
d. They have less egalitarian attitudes about gender roles.

19. Families under economic stress are:
a. more likely to have good cooperation with regard to parenting.
b. less likely to monitor children's activities.
c. more likely to monitor children's activities.
d. likely to have resilient children.

20. Research has found which of the following regarding joint custody?
a. There can be a few advantages in some cases.
b. Children enjoy it.
c. Most parents are cheerful about it.
d. Most parents prefer it.

21. Leaving a child out of a group is:
a. Relational aggression.
b. Hostile aggression.
c. Instrumental aggression.
d. All of the above.

22. Bullying tends to _____ during middle childhood.
a. increase
b. decrease
c. remain stable
d. disappear

23. In middle childhood, the peer group is:
a. more important than in early childhood.
b. a factor in gauging abilities.
c. important in teaching children how to get along with others.
d. All of these.

24. A child who refuses to obey and with a negative attitude toward authority figures is more likely to have the diagnosis of:
a. School phobia.
b. Separation anxiety.
c. Conduct disorder.
d. Oppositional defiant disorder.

25. A child who sets fires, harms others, and feels no remorse is likely to have the diagnosis of _____ disorder.
a. Obsessive compulsive
b. Oppositional defiant
c. Conduct
d. Depressive

Short Essay Questions

These short essay questions are based on the Checkpoints in the chapter. Answer each question as completely and succinctly as possible. Check your answers by reviewing the part of the chapter that covers the Guidepost listed with each question.

1. Briefly summarize the factors that influence a child's adjustment to divorce. (See Guidepost 2.)

2. Describe research support for and against the idea that children from traditional families are better adjusted than are children from nontraditional families. (See Guidepost 2.)

3. How do the stresses of modern life affect children, and what enables resilient children to withstand them? (See Guidepost 6.)

4. Summarize the most common forms of aggressive behavior in middle childhood, and discuss the influences that specifically contribute to aggressive behaviors. (See Guidepost 4.)

5. Describe the changes that take place in the parent-child relationship during middle childhood. (see Guidepost 2.)

Organize It!

Making lists is a fun and useful way to categorize information in your mind. After making each list, think of ways to memorize it so that you have immediate recall. Singing a list, dancing while you recite it, or simply saying it in a rhythmic pattern as you are walking, driving, or jogging allows your brain to store the information in easily retrievable form. Try it!

1. List and describe four indicators of emotional growth in middle childhood. (See Guidepost 1.)

   1.

   2.

   3.

   4.

2. Briefly list and describe three gender differences in response to maternal employment. (See Guidepost 2.)

   1.

   2.

   3.

3. List and briefly describe eight common emotional disorders of childhood. (See Guidepost 5.)

   1.

   2.

   3.

   4.

   5.

   6.

   7.

   8.

4. List and briefly describe Selman's four stages of friendship. (See Guidepost 3.)

    1.

    2.

    3.

    4.

5. List and briefly describe five protective factors that have been identified for resilient children (See Guidepost 6.)

    1.

    2.

    3.

    4.

    5.

6. List the five peer status groups related to popularity. (See Guidepost 3.)

    1.

    2.

    3.

    4.

    5.

Critical Thinking Questions

These questions may be used in small group discussions or as extra-credit reports, if your instructor accepts extra credit reports.

1. If you were infertile, would you wish to adopt a child? Why or why not? Consider in your answer the age of a potential adopted child, as well as the racial and cultural characteristics you would find important in your decision.

2. Is it a good idea to stay married until young children are grown, and then get a divorce? Or should you divorce when the problems begin?

3. What do you think causes the violent outbreaks in middle childhood and young adolescence that have been in the news during the past several years? What are some contributing factors?

Answer Keys

True/False Self-Test

1.	T	GP 1
2.	F	GP 1
3.	T	GP 1
4.	T	GP 1
5.	T	GP 2
6.	T	GP 2
7.	F	GP 2
8.	F	GP 2
9.	T	GP 2
10.	T	GP 4
11.	F	GP 4
12.	F	GP 2
13.	T	GP 2
14.	F	GP 2
15.	F	GP 5
16.	F	GP 2
17.	T	GP 5
18.	T	GP 2
19.	T	GP 2
20.	T	GP 2
21.	T	GP 3
22.	F	GP 3
23.	F	GP 4
24.	T	GP 3
25.	F	GP 5

Multiple-Choice Self-Test

1.	b	GP 1
2.	b	GP 1
3.	c	GP 1
4.	b	GP 2
5.	a	GP 2
6.	d	GP 2
7.	b	GP 2
8.	d	GP 4
9.	a	GP 1
10.	d	GP 1
11.	b	GP 2
12.	b	GP 2
13.	d	GP 2
14.	c	GP 2
15.	a	GP 2
16.	b	GP 2
17.	d	GP 2
18.	a	GP 2
19.	b	GP 2
20.	a	GP 2
21.	a	GP 4
22.	a	GP 4
23.	d	GP 3
24.	d	GP 5
25.	c	GP 5

PART 5: ADOLESCENCE

CHAPTER 11: PHYSICAL AND COGNITIVE DEVELOPMENT IN ADOLESCENCE

Chapter 11, which opens Part 5 of the text, introduces you to the period of adolescence. Physical growth and other changes are rapid and profound as individual reach reproductive maturity. Major health risks arise from behavioral issues, such as eating disorders and drug abuse. The ability to think abstractly and to use scientific reasoning develops at this time, although immature thinking persists in some attitudes. Education becomes focused on preparation for college or vocations.

Guideposts for Study

1. What is adolescence, when does it begin and end, and what opportunities and risks does it entail?

2. What physical changes do adolescents experience, and how do these changes affect them psychologically?

3. What brain developments occur during adolescence, and how do they affect adolescent behavior?

4. What are some common health problems in adolescence, and how can they be prevented?

5. How do adolescents' thinking and use of language differ from younger children's?

6. On what basis do adolescents make moral judgments?

7. What factors affect adolescents' school success and their educational and vocational planning and preparation?

Detailed Chapter Outline with Key Terms

I. ADOLESCENCE: A DEVELOPMENTAL TRANSITION
   - **Adolescence**: Developmental transition between childhood and adulthood entailing major physical, cognitive, and psychosocial changes.
   - **Puberty**: Process that leads to sexual maturity and reproductive ability.
   - *Pubescence:* Term meaning puberty.
   A. Adolescence as a social construction
   B. Adolescence: A Time of Opportunities and Risks
PHYSICAL DEVELOPMENT
II. PUBERTY: THE END OF CHILDHOOD
   A. How Puberty Begins: Hormonal Changes
      - Dehydroepiandrosterone (DHEA): Hormone secreted by the adrenal glands that plays a part in growth at puberty.
      - **Adrenarche:** The maturing of the adrenal glands.
      - **Gonadarche:** The maturing of the sex organs.

B. Timing, Sequence, and Signs of Puberty and Sexual
   1. Primary and Secondary Sex Characteristics
      - **Primary sex characteristics**: Organs directly related to reproduction.
      - **Secondary sex characteristics**: Physiological signs of sexual maturation, such as breast development and body hair growth, that do not involve sex organs.
      - *Areolae:* The pigmented areas surrounding the nipples, which enlarge during puberty.
   2. Signs of Puberty
   3. **The adolescent growth spurt**: Sharp increase in height and weight that precedes sexual maturity.
   4. Signs of Sexual Maturity: Sperm Production and Menstruation
      - **Spermarche**: Boy's first ejaculation.
      - *Nocturnal emission:* An involuntary ejaculation of semen (commonly referred to as a *wet dream*) that happens at night in males.
      - *Menstruation:* The monthly shedding of tissue from the lining of the womb.
      - **Menarche**: Girl's first menstruation.
   5. Influences on and Effects of Timing on Puberty
      - **Secular trend**: Trend that can be seen only by observing several generations, such as the trend toward earlier attainment of adult height and sexual maturity, which began a century ago.

III. THE ADOLESCENT BRAIN
      - *Socioemotional network:* The brain network that is sensitive to social and emotional stimuli.
      - *Cognitive-Control network:* the brain network that regulates responses to stimuli.

IV. PHYSICAL AND MENTAL HEALTH
   A. Physical Activity
   B. Sleep Needs and Problems
      - *Melatonin:* A hormone secreted by the pineal gland, which promotes sleep.
   C. Nutrition and Eating Disorders
      1. Obesity
      2. Body Image and Eating Disorders
      - **Body image**: Descriptive and evaluative beliefs about one's appearance.

3. Anorexia nervosa
      - **Anorexia nervosa**: Eating disorder characterized by self-starvation.

4. Bulimia Nervosa
      - **Bulimia nervosa**: Eating disorder in which a person regularly eats huge quantities of food and then purges the body by taking laxatives, inducing vomiting, fasting, or exercising excessively.
      - *Binge eating disorder:* Frequent bingeing without subsequent fasting, exercise, or vomiting.
   5. Treatment and Outcomes of Anorexia and Bulimia
   D. Use and Abuse of Drugs
      - **Substance Abuse:** Harmful use of alcohol or drugs that last more than one month during which a person continues to use the substance after knowingly being harmed by it or using it in a hazardous situation.

- **Substance Dependence:** Addiction, which may be physiological, psychological, or both.
  1. Trends in Drug Use
  2. Risk Factors for Drug Abuse
  3. Alcohol, Marijuana, and Tobacco
  E. Depression
  F. Death in Adolescence
  1. Deaths from Vehicle Accidents and Firearms
  2. Suicide

COGNITIVE DEVELOPMENT
V. ASPECTS OF COGNITIVE MATURATION
  A. Piaget's stage of Formal Operations
  - **formal operations**: Piaget's final stage of cognitive development, characterized by the ability to think abstractly.
  1. **Hypothetical-deductive reasoning**: Ability believed by Piaget to accompany the state of formal operations, to develop, consider, and test hypotheses.
  2. Evaluating Piaget's Theory
  Metacognition: Awareness and monitoring of one's own mental processes and strategies.
  B. Elkind: Immature Characteristics of Adolescent Thought
  Six Characteristics of Immature Adolescent Thought:
  1. Idealism and Criticalness: Adolescent vision of an ideal world
  2. Argumentativeness: Adolescent desire to try out reasoning skills with arguments.
  3. Indecisiveness: Adolescent's lack of effective strategies for choosing between alternatives.
  4. Apparent Hypocrisy: Adolescent's difficulty in recognizing the difference in an ideal and making the sacrifices necessary to achieve the ideal.
  5. Self-consciousness
  - **Imaginary audience**: Elkind's term for an observer who exists only in an adolescent's mind and is as concerned with the adolescent's thoughts and actions as the adolescent is.
  6. Specialness and Invulnerability
  - **Personal fable**: Elkind's term for the conviction that one is special, unique, and not subject to the rules that govern the rest of the world.
  C. Changes in Information Processing in Adolescence
  1. *Structural Change*: changes in information-processing capacity and the increasing amount of knowledge stored in long-term memory.
  - **Declarative knowledge:** factual knowledge that a person has acquired
  - **Procedural knowledge:** skills that a person has acquired.
  - **Conceptual knowledge:** understanding of information that a person has acquired.
  2. *Functional Change:* process for obtaining, handling, and retaining information.
  C. Language Development
  - Social Perspective-taking: The ability to understand another person's point of view and level of knowledge and speak accordingly.

D. Moral Reasoning: Kohlberg's Theory
  1. Kohlberg's Levels and Stages
      • Level I: **Preconventional morality**: First level, in which control is external.
      • Level II: **Conventional morality (or morality of conventional role conformity)**: Second level, in which standards of authority figures are internalized.
      • Level III: **Postconventional morality (or morality of autonomous moral principles)**: Third level, in which people follow internally held moral principles and can decide among conflicting moral standards.
  2. Evaluating Kohlberg's Theory
      a. Influence of Parents, Peers, and Culture
E. Gilligan's Theory: An Ethic of Care
F. Prosocial Behavior and Volunteer Activity
VI. EDUCATIONAL AND VOCATIONAL ISSUES
  A. Influences on School Achievement
    1. Student Motivation and Self-Efficacy
        • *Self-efficacy:* Belief in one's own mastery of situations, such as mastery of academic material.
    3. Importance of SES and Related Family Characteristics
    4. Gender
    5. Parenting Styles, Ethnicity, and Peer Influence
        • *Authoritative parenting:* Baumrind's parenting style that urges adolescents to look at both sides of issues and welcomes participation in family decisions.
        • *Authoritarian parenting:* Baumrind's parenting style that tells adolescent not to argue or question parents.
        • *Permissive parenting:* Baumrind's parenting style that shows indifference.
        6. The school
  B. Dropping Out of High School
      Active engagement: The attention, interest, investment and effort students expend in the work of school.
  C. Preparing for Higher Education or Vocations
    1. Influences on Students' Aspirations
    2. Guiding Students Not Bound for College
    3. Adolescents in the Workplace

147

True/False Self-Test

Place a T or an F in the appropriate space. These questions are taken from the chapter content, tables, key terms, Guideposts for Study, and Checkpoints.

1. ____ The concept of adolescence is a social construction.

2. ____ The beginning and the end of adolescence is clearly marked in Western societies.

3. ____ Puberty is triggered by hormonal changes, which may affect moods and behavior.

4. ____ Risky behavior patterns do not emerge until late adolescence.

5. ____ Research has shown that active engagement is an important factor in decreasing school drop-outs.

6. ____ During puberty, both boys and girls undergo an adolescent growth spurt.

7. ____ Self-efficacy has minimal impact upon educational and vocational goals.

8. ____ Adolescents are more likely than young children to get regular medical care.

9. ____ The ethnic groups with the lowest dropout rates are poor Hispanic and African-American students.

10. ____ The principal signs of sexual maturity are production of sperm for males and menstruation for females.

11. ____ Most high school students engage in vigorous physical activity.

12. ____ Many adolescents do not get enough sleep because the high school schedule is out of sync with their circadian timing system.

13. ____ Substance abuse is less common among adolescents today than in recent years.

14. ____ Anorexia and bulimia affect mostly girls.

15. ____ The three leading causes of death among adolescents are accidents, homicide, and suicide.

16. ____ Outcomes for patients with bulimia tend to be better than for those with anorexia.

17. ____ Alcohol, cocaine, and heroin are the gateway drugs popular with adolescents.

18. ____ Adolescence is a time of development of abstract thought, according to Piaget.

19. ___ The ability to think abstractly has emotional implications.

20. ___ Many late adolescents and adults seem incapable of abstract thought as Piaget defined it.

21. ___ The personal fable and imaginary audience suggested by Elkind disappear in late adolescence.

22. ___ Kohlberg has described 10 levels of moral reasoning.

23. ___ According to Kohlberg, some people never reach the third level of moral reasoning.

24. ___ Neither Piaget nor Kohlberg considered parents important to children's moral development.

25. ___ According to Gilligan, women may see morality in terms of responsibility to show care and avoid harm.

Multiple-Choice Self-Test

Circle the letter of the best answer. These questions are based on many aspects of the chapter content, in no particular order.

1. Puberty begins:
a. in the sixth grade.
b. in high school.
c. with a sharp increase in the production of sex hormones.
d. None of these.

2. Adolescent brains appear to process emotional information in the _____ of the brain whereas adults process this information in the _____ of the brain.
a. frontal lobes, pariental lobes.
b. amygdala, frontal lobes.
c. frontal lobes, hypothalamus.
d. pituitary, frontal cortex.

3. Secretion of the sex hormones appears to be related to:
a. reaching a critical weight level.
b. maturation of the adrenal glands.
c. increased levels of DHEA.
d. All of these.

4. Alcohol, marijuana, and tobacco are called gateway drugs because:
a. teens are usually introduced to the drugs by their peers.
b. their use often leads to use of more addictive substances.
c. their use typically leads to destructive behaviors.
d. teens who use them are teetering on the fringes of society.

5. The development of facial and axillary hair and voice changes are considered to be:
a. primary sex characteristics.
b. secondary sex characteristics.
c. indiscriminate sex characteristics
d. All of these.

6. The timing of onset of puberty for females has some connection to:
a. ethnicity with White girls having their periods earlier than African-American girls..
b. girls' interactions with their fathers.
c. having strong, affectionate relationships with their mothers.
d. girls' secretion of pheromones.

7. Puberty begins earlier for:
a. girls than for boys.
b. boys than for girls.
c. boys who are raised by single mothers.
d. boys who are raised in the countryside.

8. With respect to formal operational thought:
a. research has demonstrated that normal adolescents and adults rely primarily on this type of thinking.
b. the role of the situation in influencing adolescents' thinking has been well documented.
c. it can be clearly delineated from concrete operational thought.
d. Piaget's analysis of its development may not have given enough credit to experiences and wisdom.

9. The secular trend that began about 100 years ago in Japan, the United States, and Western Europe includes:
a. a lowering of the age when puberty begins.
b. a raising of the age when puberty begins.
c. increased height in males only.
d. decreased weight in females only.

10. The Cowens talk to their teenage son about both sides of issues and encourage him to participate in family decisions. They are using the _____ parenting style.
a. authoritarian
b. authoritative
c. permissive
d. neglecting

11. Which of the following is NOT a behavior that Elkind attributes to adolescence?
a. argumentativeness
b. respect for authority figures
c. apparent hypocrisy
d. assumption of invulnerability

12. A child's choice of vocation is related to:
a. parents' attitudes and values.
b. gender and gender stereotyping.
c. the educational system.
d. All of these.

13. Who is most likely to go to college?
a. Paul who is East-Asian and has professional parents
b. Maria who has Hispanic parents who are migrant workers
c. Devon who has a single mom and is African-American
d. John, who is Caucasian and has a reading disability

14. Kohlberg's theory of moral development:
a. suggests that children whose parents use humor, praise, and ask their children's opinions show greater progress through the stages.
b. concludes that parental input and support are critical elements of developing a high sense of morality.
c. is oriented toward values that are more important to women than to men.

d. has demonstrated that people around the world progress into all three levels.

15. The majority of American educational systems favor students who:
a. think critically.
b. are creative and think "outside the box."
c. memorize easily and do well on tests.
d. All of these students should do equally well.

16. Active engagement appears to be promoted by:
a. family encouragement.
b. small class sizes.
c. a warm and supportive school environment.
d. All of these.

17. In a national survey, almost ___ of students reported seriously considering suicide during the past year.
a. 10%
b. 50%
c. 25%
d. 90%

18. The primary sex characteristics are:
a. the organs necessary for reproduction.
b. readily apparent in girls.
c. breasts in females.
d. growth of facial hair in males

19. _____ seems to help young people from disadvantaged neighborhoods do well in school.
a. Innate intelligence
b. Academic tracking
c. Authoritarian parenting
d. Social capital

20. In males, the principal sign of sexual maturity is:
a. facial hair.
b. chest hair.
c. deepened voice.
d. sperm production.

21. Perhaps the most important factor in whether a student will finish school is:
a. parenting style.
b. active engagement.
c. school resources.
d. socioeconomic status.

22. Which factors are associated with early pubertal development in girls?
a. absent father
b. cold, distant father
c. genetic influences
d. All of these.

23. Which of the following is true of most adolescents?
a. They are reasonably healthy.
b. They don't get enough sleep.
c. They don't exercise enough.
d. All of these.

24. In the morning, most teenagers are:
a. alert.
b. not alert.
c. happy and energetic.
d. ready to study.

25. After puberty, secretion of this hormone takes place later at night.
a. estrogen
b. serotonin
c. melatonin
d. testosterone

Short Essay Questions

These short essay questions are based on the Checkpoints in the chapter. Answer each question as completely and succinctly as possible. Check your answers by reviewing the part of the chapter that covers the Guidepost listed with each question.

1. Kohlberg's method of assessing moral development by evaluating participants' reactions to moral dilemmas is widely used. Does this seem like the most appropriate method? Why or why not? What would you suggest as an alternative measure? (See Guidepost 6.)

2. What are some educational practices that can help high school students do better? (See Guidepost 7.)

3. List at least three criticisms and weaknesses of Kohlberg's theory of moral development. (See Guidepost 6.)

4. Should marijuana be legal, like alcohol? Why or why not? Should there be tighter restrictions on cigarette advertising? If so, what kinds of restrictions would you favor? (See Guidepost 4.)

Organize It!

Making lists is a fun and useful way to categorize information in your mind. After making each list, think of ways to memorize it so that you have immediate recall. Singing a list, dancing while you recite it, or simply saying it in a rhythmic pattern as you are walking, driving, or jogging allows your brain to store the information in easily retrievable form. Try it!

1. List the three most common mineral deficiencies in the diets of adolescents. (See Guidepost 4.)

    1.

    2.

    3.

2. List four signs of anorexia nervosa and four signs of bulimia nervosa. (See Guidepost 4.)

    Anorexia
    1.
    2.
    3.
    4.

Bulimia

1.

2.

3.

4.

3. List four secondary sex characteristics each for boys and girls. (See Guidepost 2.)

Boys

1.

2.

3.

4.

Girls

1.

2.

3.

4.

4. List and briefly describe Elkind's six immature characteristics of adolescent thought. (See Guidepost 5.)

1.

2.

3.

4.

5.

6.

5. List the 10 risk factors associated with substance abuse. (See Guidepost 4)

1.

2.

3.

4.

5.

6.

7.

8.

9.

10.

Critical Thinking Questions

These questions may be used in small group discussions or as extra-credit reports, if your instructor agrees.

1. How might early maturation be different for girls than for boys? Late maturation?

2. Why are eating disorders so prevalent in Western cultures? What might be some ways to reduce the prevalence of eating disorders?

3. What might be some ways that parents and educators could encourage students to finish high school?

Answer Keys

True/False Self-Test

1.	T	GP 1		14.	T	GP 4
2.	F	GP 1		15.	T	GP 4
3.	T	GP 2		16.	T	GP 4
4.	F	GP 3		17.	F	GP 4
5.	T	GP 7		18.	T	GP 5
6.	T	GP 2		19.	T	GP 5
7.	F	GP 7		20.	T	GP 5
8.	F	GP 4		21.	F	GP 5
9.	F	GP 7		22.	F	GP 6
10.	T	GP 2		23.	T	GP 6
11.	F	GP 4		24.	T	GP 6
12.	T	GP 4		25.	T	GP 6
13.	T	GP 4				

Multiple-Choice Self-Test

1.	c	GP 2		14.	a	GP 6
2.	b	GP 3		15.	c	GP 6
3.	d	GP 2		16.	d	GP 7
4.	b	GP 4		17.	c	GP 4
5.	b	GP 2		18.	a	GP 2
6.	b	GP 2		19.	d	GP 7
7.	b	GP 2		20.	d	GP 2
8.	d	GP 5		21.	b	GP 7
9.	a	GP 2		22.	d	GP 2
10.	b	GP 5		23.	d	GP 4
11.	b	GP 5		24.	b	GP 4
12.	d	GP 7		25.	c	GP 4
13.	a	GP 7				

CHAPTER 12: PSYCHOSOCIAL DEVELOPMENT IN ADOLESCENCE

This chapter focuses on the search for identity in adolescence, sexuality, and relationships with family, peers, and adult society. The views of Erikson, Marcia, and Elkind are explored. Focus boxes examine the topics of preventing teen pregnancy and the youth violence epidemic in the United States.

Guideposts for Study

1. How do adolescents form an identity and what roles do gender and ethnicity play?

2. What determines sexual orientation, what sexual practices are common among adolescents, and what leads some to engage in risky sexual behavior?

3. How do adolescents relate to parents, siblings, and peers?

4. What are the root causes of antisocial behavior and juvenile delinquency, and what can be done to reduce these risks of adolescence?

Detailed Chapter Outline and Key Terms

I. THE SEARCH FOR IDENTITY
   Identity: According to Erikson, a coherent conception of the self, made up of goals, values, and beliefs to which a person is solidly committed.
   A. Erikson: Identity versus Identity Confusion
   - **Identity versus identity confusion**: Erikson's fifth crisis of psychosocial development, in which an adolescent seeks to develop a coherent sense of self by resolving the choice of an *occupation;* the adoption of *values,* and development of a satisfying *sexual identity.* Also called *identity versus role confusion.*
   - *Psychological moratorium:* In Erikson's theory, a "time-out" period that is provided by adolescence to allow young people time to search for commitments.
   - *Fidelity:* In Erikson's theory, the virtue attained in the fifth crisis, involving sustained loyalty, faith, and/or a sense of belonging to loved ones.
   B. Marcia: Identity Status—Crisis and Commitment
   - **Identity statuses**: States of ego development that depend on the presence or absence of crisis and commitment.
   - **Crisis**: A period of conscious decision making related to identity formation.
   - **Commitment**: Personal investment in an occupation or system of beliefs.
   - **Identity achievement**: Identity status that is characterized by a commitment to choices made following a crisis, a period spent in exploring alternatives.

- **Foreclosure**: Identity status in which a person who has not spent time considering alternatives (i.e., has not been in crisis) is committed to other people's plans for his or her life.
- **Moratorium**: Identity status in which a person is currently considering alternatives (in crisis) and seems headed for commitment.
- **Identity diffusion**: Identity status that is characterized by absence of commitment and lack of serious consideration of alternatives.

   C. Gender Differences in Identity Formation
   D. Ethnic Factors in Identity Formation
     Four Stages of Ethnic Identity:
     1. *Diffuse:* Little or no exploration of ethnic identity, no clear understanding of issues involved.
     2. *Foreclosed:* Little or no exploration of ethnic identity, but has positive or negative feelings about it from attitudes absorbed at home.
     3. *Moratorium:* Has begun to explore ethnic identity but is confused about what it means.
     4. *Achieved:* Has explored ethnic identity and understands and accepts it.
     Three Aspects of Racial/Ethnic Identity
     1. *Connectedness:* connection to one's own racial and ethnic group.
     2. *Awareness of racism*
     3. *Embedded Achievement: the belief that academic achievement is a part of group identity*
     Two Dimensions of Ethic Identity
- *Group esteem:* feeling good about one's ethnicity
- *Exploration of the meaning of ethnicity*
- **Cultural Socialization:** reference to parental practices that teach children about their racial and ethnic heritage, promote cultural customs and traditions, and promote racial/ethnic and cultural pride.

II. SEXUALITY
- *Sexual identity:* seeing oneself as a sexual being, recognizing one's sexual orientation, coming to terms with sexual stirrings, and forming romantic and sexual attachments.

   A. Sexual Orientation and Identity
- **Sexual orientation**: Focus of consistent sexual, romantic, and affectionate interest, whether heterosexual, homosexual, or bisexual.
- *Heterosexual:* Attracted to persons of the opposite sex.
- *Homosexual:* Attracted to persons of the same sex.
- *Bisexual:* Attracted to persons of either sex.
- *Sexual or Romantic Attraction or Arousal:* measurement of orientation though by attraction
- *Sexual Behavior:* measurement of orientation through behaviors
- *Sexual Identity:* measurement of orientation though identity.

    1. Origins of Sexual Orientation
    2. Homosexual and Bisexual Identity Development
   B. Sexual Behavior
    1. Sexual Risk Taking

2. Use of Contraceptives

3. Where Do Teenagers Get Information about Sex?

C. Sexually Transmitted Diseases (STDs)

Sexually transmitted diseases (STDs): Diseases spread by sexual contact.

D. Teenage Pregnancy and Childbearing

1. Outcomes of Teenage Pregnancy

2. Preventing Teenage Pregnancy

III. RELATIONSHIPS WITH FAMILY, PEERS, AND ADULT SOCIETY

A. Is Adolescent Rebellion a Myth?

Adolescent rebellion: Pattern of emotional turmoil, characteristic of a minority of adolescents, which may involve conflict with family, alienation from adult society, reckless behavior, and rejection of adult values.

B. Changing Time Use and Changing Relationships

C. Adolescents and Parents

1. Individuation and Family Conflict

- **Individuation:** an adolescent's struggle for autonomy and differentiation or personal identity.
- Parenting Styles and Parental Authority
- *Behavioral Control:* Control over a child's conduct
- *Psychological Control:* Control over a child's feelings, beliefs, and sense of self.
- *Psychological Autonomy:* The child's need to have their own thoughts and feelings.

4. Parental Monitoring and Adolescents' Self-disclosure

5. Family Structure and Family Atmosphere

4. Mothers' Employment and Economic Stress

D. Adolescents and Siblings

E. Adolescents and Peers

- *Dyadic:* One-to-one peer interactions
- *Cliques:* structured groups of friends who do things together.
- *Crowd:* larger grouping based upon reputation, image, or identity.

1. Friendships

2. Romantic Relationships

IV. Antisocial Behavior and Juvenile Delinquency

A. Becoming a Delinquent: Genetic and Neurological Factors

B. Becoming a Delinquent: How Family, Peer, and Community Influences Interact

- *Collective efficacy:* The strength of social connections within a neighborhood and the extent to which residents monitor or supervise each other's children.

1. Long-Term Prospects

2. Preventing and Treating Delinquency

True/False Self-Test

Place a T or an F in the appropriate space. These questions are taken from the chapter content, tables, key terms, Guideposts for Study, and Checkpoints.

1. ____ Erikson has described the psychosocial crisis of adolescence as industry versus inferiority.

2. ____ A central concern during adolescence is the search for the right marriage partner.

3. ____ Foreclosure is one of James Marcia's four identity statuses.

4. ____ Ethnicity is an unimportant part of identity.

5. ____ Adolescents who accept the plans of others as their goals are in foreclosure status.

6. ____ Erikson believed that identity and intimacy develop together for women.

7. ____ Sexual orientation appears to be influenced by peer group pressure.

8. ____ Sexual attitudes and behaviors are more liberal than in the past.

9. ____ Adolescents who are at greatest risk for sexually transmitted diseases are those who become sexually active later in life.

10. ___ Sexually transmitted diseases have become far more prevalent since the 1960s.

11. ___ In the United States, rates of teenage pregnancy and birth are climbing.

12. ___ Conflict with parents tends to be more frequent in early adolescence and more intense in middle adolescence.

13. ___ In Asian and European cultures, adolescents are more likely to be in conflict with mothers than with fathers.

14. ___ Authoritative parenting is most often associated with positive outcomes.

15. ___ Economic stress does not affect relationships in two-parent families.

16. ___ Most juvenile delinquents grow up to be law-abiding citizens.

17. ___ Relationships with siblings tend to become more distant and based upon power during adolescence than during middle childhood.

18. ___ In three out of four assaults or murders by young people, the perpetrators are female.

19. ___ Violence and antisocial behavior have roots in childhood.

20. ___ Children who are raised in a rejecting or coercive atmosphere or in an overly permissive or chaotic one tend to show aggressive behavior, and the hostility they evoke in others increases their own aggression.

21. ___ Adolescents are more likely to turn violent if they have witnessed or have been victims of violence, such as physical abuse or neighborhood fights.

22. ___ Peer interactions can stimulate moral growth if the peer climate is positive.

23. ___ STDs are more likely to develop undetected in men than in women.

24. ___ Friendships become less intimate and supportive in adolescence than in middle childhood, especially among girls.

25. ___ In Marcia's terminology, commitment is a personal investment in an occupation or system of beliefs.

Multiple-Choice Self-Test

Circle the letter of the best answer. These questions are based on many aspects of the chapter content, in no particular order.

1. The chief task of adolescence, according to Erikson, is:
a. trust vs. mistrust.
b. identity vs. identity confusion.
c. autonomy vs. shame and doubt.
d. industry vs. guilt.

2. According to Erikson, adolescents form their identity by:
a. modeling themselves after other people.
b. following their parents' wishes.
c. getting an education.
d. modifying and synthesizing earlier identifications.

3. Cliquishness and intolerance of differences are:
a. abnormal and extreme reactions.
b. hallmarks of autism.
c. seen mainly in Asian girls.
d. normal adolescent defenses against identity confusion.

4. Identity forms as young people resolve the following:
a. choice of an occupation
b. adoption of values to believe in and live by
c. development of a satisfying sexual identity
d. All of these.

5. Erikson's theory describes:
a. male identity development as the norm.
b. female identity development as the norm.
c. males as achieving identity through intimacy.
d. females as achieving identity through career choices.

6. Joseph accepts that he is a Catholic because his entire family is Catholic, and he has never questioned this part of his identity. Which status of identity formation describes Joseph?
a. moratorium
b. foreclosure
c. identity achievement
d. identity diffusion

7. An adolescent who has no commitments to serious goals, and has only superficial friendships is in:
a. identity diffusion.
b. moratorium.
c. foreclosure.
d. identity achievement.

8. Most research supports Erikson's view that, for women:
a. identity and intimacy are unrelated.
b. intimacy and identity develop together.
c. more time is spent in identity diffusion.
d. more time is spent in foreclosure.

9. During adolescence, self-esteem develops largely:
a. in the context of relationships with parents.
b. in the context of relationships with peers.
c. as a result of employment.
d. as a function of academic excellence.

10. Identity formation is especially complicated for:
a. young people in minority groups.
b. girls.
c. boys.
d. All of these.

11. Latonya has begun to explore her ethnicity but is confused about what it means. She is in which stage of ethnic identity?
a. diffuse
b. achieved
c. foreclosed
d. moratorium

12. The urgent awareness of _____ is an important aspect of identity formation.
a. self-esteem
b. gender
c. ethnicity
d. sexuality

13. Homosexuality is:
a. considered a mental illness.
b. a consequence of poor parental supervision.
c. the result of imbalanced hormones.
d. no longer considered a mental disorder.

14. Which of the following has been revealed by research on the origins of sexual orientation?
a. Orientation may be at least partially genetic.
b. It may be influenced by a complex prenatal process.
c. Sexual orientation may be influenced by biological, psychological, and social influences.
d. All of these.

15. The sexual revolution has:
a. brought more acceptance of homosexuality.
b. reduced tolerance of homosexuality.
c. not affected attitudes about homosexuality.
d. brought more tension and confusion.

16. Some factors related to delinquency include:
a. early entrance into puberty.
b. poor school performance.
c. high SES.
d. authoritative parenting.

17. The best safeguard for sexually active teens is:
a. regular use of condoms.
b. regular church attendance.
c. private school.
d. home schooling.

18. Adolescents who do not use contraceptives, or who use them irregularly or ineffectively, tend to:
a. be in their early teens.
b. be in their late teens.
c. have high self-esteem.
d. be very experienced with sex.

19. Teenagers in the "high-risk group" for unsafe sexual behavior are more likely than those at lower risk to:
a. have low grades.
b. be frequent drinkers.
c. have been abused by their parents.
d. All of these.

20. Many teenagers obtain their unrealistic information about sex from:
a. school classes.
b. the media.
c. peers.
d. parents.

21. Teenage pregnancy rates in the United States are:
a. the lowest in six decades.
b. many times higher than in other industrialized countries.
c. the same as in Sweden.
d. lower than most industrialized countries.

22. Abstinence-only sex education programs:
a. do not lead to more sexual activity.
b. increase sexual activity among preteens.
c. do not delay sexual activity.
d. are highly successful

23. Karina is 14. Which whom is she most likely to prefer to spend her Saturdays?
a. her mother
b. her friends.
c. her father.
d. her siblings.

24. Full-fledged teenage rebellion is:
a. a normal result of hormonal changes.
b. normal.
c. uncommon even in Western societies.
d. None of these.

25. The experience of adolescence as a period of "storm and stress" is:
a. universal.
b. not universal.
c. common to American teenagers.
d. mainly biological in source.

Short Essay Questions

These short essay questions are based on the Checkpoints in the chapter. Answer each question as completely and succinctly as possible. Check your answers by reviewing the part of the chapter that covers the Guidepost listed with each question.

1. List and describe at least three theories regarding origins of sexual orientation and the research related to each. (See Guidepost 2.)

2. Summarize current trends in teenage pregnancy and birth rates in the United States. Include in your discussion the problems and outcomes of teenage pregnancy and your suggestions for preventing teen pregnancies. (See Guidepost 2.)

3. Identify age, gender, and cultural differences in how young people spend their time, and discuss the significance of these differences. (See Guidepost 3.)

4. Describe the important features of girls' and boys' friendships in adolescence. (See Guidepost 3.)

Organize It!

Making lists is a fun and useful way to categorize information in your mind. After making each list, think of ways to memorize it so that you have immediate recall. Singing a list, dancing while you recite it, or simply saying it in a rhythmic pattern as you are walking, driving, or jogging allows your brain to store the information in easily retrievable form. Try it!

1. List Marcia's four types of identity status. (See Guidepost 1.)

    1.

    2.

    3.

    4.

2. List the eight most common sexually transmitted diseases. (See Table 12-4 and Guidepost 4.)

   1.

   2.

   3.

   4.

   5.

   6.

   7.

   8.

3. List the three major issues involved in identity formation, according to Erikson. (See Guidepost 1.)

   1.

   2.

   3.

4. List the five myths associated with youth violence. (See Table for Box 12.2 and Guidepost 4.)

   1.

   2.

   3.

   4.

   5.

5. List the risk factors associated with chronic delinquency. (See Guidepost 4).

   1.

   2.

3.

4.

Critical Thinking Questions

These questions may be used in small group discussions or, if your instructor agrees, as extra-credit reports.

1. Which of Marcia's identity statuses do you think you fit into as an adolescent? Has your identity status changed since then? If so, how?

2. If you learned that your son or daughter was homosexual, how do you think you would feel? What would you say or do?

3. If you have siblings, how are your relationships with them different now from what they were when you were an adolescent?

4. Should the media be held responsible for the prevalence of violence portrayed in the various formats (e.g., television, movies)? What can parents do to help prevent violence in their adolescent children?

Answer Keys

True/False Self-Test

1. F	GP 1	
2. F	GP 1	
3. T	GP 1	
4. F	GP 1	
5. T	GP 1	
6. T	GP 1	
7. F	GP 2	
8. T	GP 2	
9. F	GP 2	
10. T	GP 2	
11. F	GP 2	
12. T	GP 3	
13. T	GP 3	

14. T	GP 3
15. F	GP 3
16. T	GP 4
17. F	GP 3
18. F	GP 4
19. T	GP 4
20. T	GP 4
21. T	GP 3
22. T	GP 4
23. F	GP 2
24. F	GP 3
25. T	GP 1

Multiple-Choice Self-Test

1. b	GP 1
2. d	GP 1
3. d	GP 1
4. d	GP 1
5. a	GP 1
6. b	GP 1
7. a	GP 1
8. b	GP 1
9. b	GP 1
10. a	GP 1
11. d	GP 1
12. d	GP 1
13. d	GP 2

14. d	GP 2
15. a	GP 2
16. b	GP 4
17. a	GP 2
18. a	GP 2
19. d	GP 2
20. b	GP 2
21. a	GP 2
22. c	GP 2
23. b	GP 3
24. c	GP 3
25. b	GP 4

PART 6: YOUNG ADULTHOOD

CHAPTER 13: PHYSICAL AND COGNITIVE DEVELOPMENT IN EMERGING AND YOUNG ADULTHOOD

This chapter introduces Part 6 of the text. The chapter explores physical development, cognitive development, moral development, education, and work. The focus boxes examine assisted reproductive technology and the development of faith across the life span.

Guideposts for Study

1. What does it mean to be an adult, and what factors affect the timing of entrance to adulthood.

2. In what physical condition is the typical young adult, and what factors affect health and well-being?

3. What are some sexual and reproductive issues at this time of life?

4. What is distinctive about adult thought?

5. How does moral reasoning develop?

6. How do emerging adults make the transition to higher education and work, and how do these experiences affect cognitive development?

Detailed Chapter Outline with Key Terms

EMERGING ADULTHOOD
- Sexual maturation: ability to reproduce.
- Cognitive maturity: capacity for abstract thought.
- Sociological definitions of adulthood: self-supporting, have chosen a career, have formed significant or romantic partnerships, or have started a family.
- Psychological maturity: forming one's identity, becoming independent of parents, developing a sense of values, and forming relationships.
- **Emerging adulthood:** A time when young people are no longer adolescents but have not yet become fully adult.

PHYSICAL DEVELOPMENT

I. HEALTH
   A. Health Status and Health Issues
   B. Genetic Influences on Health
   C. Behavioral Influences on Health and Fitness
      1. Diet and Nutrition
      2. Obesity/Overweight
      3. Physical Activity

4. Sleep
5. Smoking
6. Alcohol Use
D. Indirect Influences on Health and Fitness
  1. Socioeconomic Status and Race/Ethnicity
  2. Relationships and Health
    - *Social Integration:* Active engagement in a broad range of social relationships, activities, and roles.
    - *Social Support:* Material, informational, and psychological resources derived from the social network on which a person can rely for help in coping with stress.
  3. Mental Health Problems
    a. Alcoholism
    - **Alcoholism:** alcohol dependence is a physical condition characterized by compulsive drinking which a person is unable to control.
    b. Drug Use and Abuse
    c. Antisocial Behavior
    d. Depression
II. SEXUAL AND REPRODUCTIVE ISSUES
  A. Sexual Behavior and Attitudes
  B. Menstrual Disorders
    - **Premenstrual syndrome (PMS)**: Disorder producing symptoms of physical discomfort and emotional tension during the one to two weeks before a menstrual period.
  C. Sexually Transmitted Diseases (STDs)
  D. Infertility
    - **Infertility**: Inability to conceive after 12 to 18 months of trying.

COGNITIVE DEVELOPMENT

III. PERSPECTIVES ON ADULT COGNITION
  A. Beyond Piaget: New Ways of Thinking in Adulthood
    1.Reflective Thinking
      - **Reflective Thinking:** A complex form of cognition defined by John Dewey that uses "active, persistent, and careful consideration" of information.
    2. Postformal Thought
    - **Postformal Thought**: Higher stage of adult cognition
    - *Seven Criteria of Postformal Thought:*
      1. *Shifting gears:* Ability to shift back and forth between the abstract and the practical.
      2. *Problem definition:* Ability to define a problem as falling within a class or category of logical problems and define its parameters.
      3. *Process*-produce shift: Ability to see that a problem can be solved either through general application to similar problems or through a concrete solution to a particular problem.
      4. *Pragmatism:* Ability to choose the best of several possible solutions and to recognize the criteria for choosing.

5. *Multiple solutions:* Awareness that most problems have more than one cause and more than one solution, with some solutions more likely to work than others.
6. *Awareness of a paradox:* Recognition that a problem or solution involves inherent conflict.
7. *Self-referential thought:* A person's awareness that he or she must be the judge of which logic to use.

B. Emotional Intelligence
- **Emotional Intelligence**: In Salovey's and Mayer's terminology, ability to understand and regulate emotions; an important component of effective, intelligent behavior.
- *Self-awareness:* A competency relying on emotional intelligence (EI), in which a person is aware of emotions and is self-confident and an accurate assessor of self.
- *Self-management:* A competency relying on emotional intelligence (EI), in which a person has self-control, adaptability, and a drive to achieve among other qualities.
- *Social awareness:* A competency relying on emotional intelligence (EI), in which a person has empathy and is oriented toward helping others.
- *Relationship management:* A competency relying on emotional intelligence (EI), in which a person can develop others, exert influence, communicate effectively, and be a good leader.

IV. MORAL REASONING
  A. Culture and Moral Reasoning
  B. Gender and Moral Reasoning

V. EDUCATION AND WORK
  A. The College Transition
    1. Adjusting to College
    2. Cognitive Growth in College
       - *Rigidity:* Rigid ideas about truth in which a person cannot conceive of any answer but the "right" one.
       - *Flexibility:* Ideas about truth where all knowledge and values are viewed as relative.
       - *Freely Chosen Commitments:* Highest level of thinking according to Perry.
       - *Commitment within Relativism:* When a young adult is able to make his or her own judgments and choose his or her own beliefs and values despite uncertainty and the recognition of other valid possibilities.
    3. Completing College
  B. Entering the World of Work
    1. Cognitive Growth at Work
    2. Combining Work and Schooling
    3. Cognitive Growth at Work
       - **Substantive complexity**: Degree to which a person's work requires thought and independent judgment.
       - **Spillover hypothesis**: Hypothesis that a positive correlation exists between intellectuality of work and of leisure activities because of a carryover of learning from work to nonwork activities.
    4. Smoothing the Transition to the Workplace

True/False Self-Test

Place a T or an F in the appropriate space. These questions are taken from the chapter content, tables, key terms, Guideposts for Study, and Checkpoints.

1. ____ The typical young adult is in good condition; physical and sensory abilities are usually excellent.

2. ____ Social relationships, especially marriage, tend to be associated with physical and mental health.

3. ____ Alcoholism is not a major health problem of young adults.

4. ____ Homicide is the leading cause of death for young adults.

5. ____ Men tend to live longer than women do, in part for biological reasons.

6. ____ Emerging adulthood is the transitional period between adolescence and the mid-20s.

7. ____ Emotional intelligence may play an important part in intelligent behavior and life success.

8. ____ According to Lawrence Kohlberg, moral reasoning depends entirely on genetics.

9. ____ Experience may be interpreted differently in various cultural contexts.

10. ____ Carol Gilligan proposed that women have moral concerns and perspectives that are not tapped in Kohlberg's theory.

11. ____ Sexual maturity typically occurs in the late 20s.

12. ____ According to Perry, college students' thinking tends to progress from flexibility to rigidity.

13. ____ Research has found a relationship between substantive complexity of work and cognitive growth.

14. ____ According to the spillover hypothesis, people who do more complex work tend to engage in more intellectually demanding leisure activities.

15. ____ Most infertility is associated with female reproductive problems.

16. ____ Worldwide, women tend to earn less than men do, and they often do low-paid, low-status work.

17. ___ In developed countries, literacy is directly linked to occupational status and income.

18. ___ A person is considered to be an adult when sexual maturation occurs.

19. ___ An increasing number of older women are returning to school.

20. ___ Postformal thought is flexible, reflective, and relativistic.

21. ___ Shifting gears, pragmatism, multiple causality, and awareness of paradox are all part of Sinnott's criteria of postformal thought.

22. ___ The sexual double standard has disappeared and men and women are judged the same regarding sexual behavior.

23. ___ According to Kohlberg, the first level of moral reasoning is postconventional morality.

24. ___ Emotional intelligence refers to a person's mental health diagnosis.

25. ___ According to Gilligan, a woman's central moral dilemma is the conflict between her own needs and those of others.

Multiple-Choice Self-Test

Circle the letter of the best answer. These questions are based on many aspects of the chapter content, in no particular order.

1. Some investigators propose a distinctively adult stage of cognition beyond formal operations, known as:
   a. pragmatism.
   b. abstraction.
   c. pessimism.
   d. postformal thought.

2. The most common cause of infertility in men is:
   a. premature ejaculation.
   b. anxiety.
   c. low sperm count.
   d. shyness.

3. Hormones of the menstrual cycle have protective effects, but can also cause health problems, notably:
   a. blockage of the fallopian tubes.
   b. premenstrual syndrome.
   c. promiscuity.
   d. hypothyroidism.

4. Which person is statistically the most likely to have the best health?
   a. a white female with a college education
   b. an African American male who completed high school
   c. a Hispanic male with a ninth grade education
   d. All of these.

5. Globally, most HIV-infected adults are:
   a. homosexual.
   b. heterosexual.
   c. IV drug users.
   d. people who have received transfusions.

6. The leading cause of death for U.S. adults under 44 years old is:
   a. accidents.
   b. AIDS.
   c. heart disease.
   d. cancer.

7. The active engagement in social relationships, activities, and roles is called:
   a. Social support.
   b. Social integration.
   c. Social intelligence.
   d. mythic-faith stage.

8. According to Perry, college students' thinking tends to progress in which order?
   a. rigid, flexible, freely chosen commitments
   b. flexible, rigid, freely chosen commitments
   c. freely chosen commitments, rigid, flexible
   d. freely chosen commitments, flexible, rigid

9. Which of the following is true of emotional intelligence?
   a. As a distinct construct, it is controversial and hard to measure.
   b. EI may play an important part in intelligent behavior.
   c. It may play an important role in life success.
   d. All of these.

10. Physical activity appears to:
a. strengthen the heart and lungs.
b. maintain normal weight.
c. reduce risks of diabetes, cancer, and osteroporosis.
d. All of these.

11. The leading, preventable, cause of death among adults is:
a. alcohol.
b. sexually transmitted disease.
c. smoking.
d. lack of sleep.

12. Antisocial behaviors tend to _____ in adulthood.
a. decrease
b. increase
c. remain stable
d. disappear

13. Postformal thinking is:
a. black and white.
b. relativistic.
c. polarized.
d. rigid.

14. Thought in adulthood often:
a. is flexible, open, and adaptive.
b. draws on intuition and emotion.
c. applies the fruits of experience to ambiguous situations.
d. All of these.

15. Shifting gears, multiple causality, multiple solutions, pragmatism, and awareness of paradox are all proposed aspects of what type of thinking?
a. componential
b. reintegrative
c. postformal
d. tacit knowledge

16. Recognition that a problem or solution involves inherent conflict ("Doing this will give him what he wants, but it will only make him unhappy in the end.") is known as:
a. pragmatism.
b. awareness of paradox.
c. shifting gears.
d. multiple causality, multiple solutions.

17. A couple is said to have infertility after _____ months of trying to conceive.
a. 2
b. 12
c. 24
d. 48

18. Self-management, management of tasks, and management of others are all part of:
a. tacit knowledge.
b. crisis orientation.
c. emotional intelligence.
d. None of these.

19. Fowler's theory has been criticized for:
a. underestimating the maturity of a simple, solid, unquestioning faith.
b. findings that may over-represent people of above average intelligence and education.
c. overlooking the adaptive value of conventional religious belief for many older adults.
d. All of these.

20. Gilligan's first level of moral development in women is:
a. goodness as self-sacrifice.
b. orientation of individual survival.
c. goodness to truth.
d. morality of nonviolence.

21. A woman who assesses her decisions not on the basis of how others will react to them, but on her intentions and the consequences of her actions is in which of Gilligan's levels of moral development?
a. level 1
b. level 2
c. level 3
d. None of these.

22. With regard to postsecondary education, socioeconomic status:
a. plays a major part in access.
b. has no impact on access.
c. is used to "weed out" potential students.
d. None of these.

23. Nearly _____ of U.S. adults are illiterate.
a. half
b. one-fourth
c. one-fifth
d. three-quarters

24. Compared to high-school graduates those holding bachelor's degrees generally make:
a. nearly twice as much money.
b. nearly half as much money.
c. about the same amount of money.
d. nearly three times as much money.

25. The completion rate for students in college is:
a. 1 in 4.
b. 2 in 4.
c. 3 in 4.
d. 4 in 4.

Short Essay Questions

These short essay questions are based on the Checkpoints in the chapter. Answer each question as completely and succinctly as possible. Check your answers by reviewing the part of the chapter that covers the Guidepost listed with each question.

1. Discuss how relationships, especially marriage, affect mental and physical health. (See Guidepost 2.)

2. Compare and contrast at least three theoretical views on moral reasoning. (See Guidepost 5.)

3. State Gilligan's original position on gender differences in moral reasoning and how it differs from Kohlberg's theory on moral reasoning. (See Guidepost 5.)

4. Tell how attending college, and working while in college, can affect cognitive development. (See Guidepost 6.)

5. Explain the relationship between substantive complexity of work and cognitive development. (See Guidepost 6.)

Organize It!

Making lists is a fun and useful way to categorize information in your mind. After making each list, think of ways to memorize it so that you have immediate recall. Singing a list, dancing while you recite it, or simply saying it in a rhythmic pattern as you are walking, driving, or jogging allows your brain to store the information in easily retrievable form. Try it!

1. List the benefits from physical activity. (See Guidepost 2.)

    1.

    2.

    3.

4.

5.

6.

7.

2. List Gilligan's three levels of women's moral development. (See Table 13.1 and Guidepost 5.)

    1.

    2.

    3.

3. List Fowler's six stages of the development of faith. (See Box 13-2.)

    1.

    2.

    3.

    4.

    5.

    6.

4. List and briefly describe six means of assisted reproduction. (See Box 13-1.)

    1.

    2.

    3.

    4.

    5.

6.

5. List the eight suggestions to smooth the transition from school to the workplace. (See Guidepost 6.)

    1.

    2.

    3.

    4.

    5.

    6.

    7.

    8.

Critical Thinking Questions

These questions can be used in small group discussions or, if your instructor agrees, for extra-credit reports.

1. What kind of lifestyle changes would you need to make to live a healthier lifestyle?

2. If you or your partner were infertile, which of the methods of assisted reproduction might you try? Why or why not?

3. Think of the most intelligent person you know. How does this person utilize the characteristics of post formal thinking?

4. Which, if either, do you consider to be the higher set moral priorities: justice and rights, or compassion and care?

5. Where do you fit in Fowler's stages of faith?

Answer Keys

True/False Self-Test

1.	T	GP 2	14.	T	GP 6
2.	T	GP 2	15.	F	GP 3
3.	F	GP 2	16.	T	GP 6
4.	F	GP 2	17.	T	GP 6
5.	F	GP 2	18.	F	GP 1
6.	T	GP 1	19.	T	GP 4
7.	T	GP 4	20.	T	GP 4
8.	F	GP 5	21.	T	GP 4
9.	T	GP 5	22.	F	GP 3
10.	T	GP 5	23.	F	GP 5
11.	F	GP 1	24.	F	GP 4
12.	F	GP 5	25.	T	GP 5
13.	T	GP 6			

Multiple-Choice Self-Test

1.	d	GP 1	14.	d	GP 4
2.	c	GP 3	15.	c	GP 4
3.	b	GP 3	16.	b	GP 4
4.	a	GP 2	17.	b	GP 3
5.	b	GP 3	18.	a	GP 6
6.	a	GP 2	19.	d	GP 5
7.	b	GP 2	20.	b	GP 5
8.	a	GP 5	21.	b	GP 5
9.	d	GP 4	22.	a	GP 4
10.	d	GP 2	23.	a	GP 6
11.	c	GP 2	24.	a	GP 6
12.	a	GP 2	25.	a	GP 6
13.	b	GP 4			

CHAPTER 14: PSYCHOSOCIAL DEVELOPMENT IN EMERGING AND YOUNG ADULTHOOD

This chapter explores four theoretical approaches to psychosocial development in young adulthood, then continues with a discussion of the foundations of intimate relationships, marital and nonmarital lifestyles, and family life.

Guideposts for Study

1. What influences varied paths to adulthood, and how do emerging adults develop a sense of adult identity and autonomous relationships with their parents?

2. Does personality change during adulthood, and if so, how?

3. How is intimacy expressed in friendship and love?

4. When and why do young adults choose to remain single, form gay or lesbian relationships, cohabit, or marry, and how satisfying and stable are those lifestyles?

5. When do most adults become parents, and how does parenthood affect a marriage?

6. What are the trends in divorce rates, and how do young adults adjust to divorce, remarriage, and stepparenthood?

Detailed Chapter Outline with Key Terms

I. EMERGING ADULTHOOD: PATTERNS AND TASKS
    A. Varied Paths to Adulthood
        1. Influences on Paths to Adulthood
    B. Identity Development in Emerging Adulthood
        1. Recentering
- **Recentering:** Process that underlies the shift to an adult identity.
  - **Stage 1:** Beginning of process with identity still centered in family of origin
  - **Stage 2:** Time during emerging adulthood when person is establishing identity away from family of origin.
  - **Stage 3:** Person moves into adulthood with commitment to a career, a partner, and possibly children.

        2. The Contemporary Moratorium
        3. Racial/Ethnic Identity Exploration
    C. Developing Adult Relationships with Parents
        1. Influences on Relationships with Parents
        2. Failure to Launch
II. PERSONALITY DEVELOPMENT: FOUR VIEWS
- **Normative-stage models**: Theoretical models that describe psychosocial development in terms of a definite sequence of age-related changes.
- **Timing-of-events model**: Theoretical model that describes adult psychosocial

development as a response to the expected or unexpected occurrence and timing of important life events.

- **Trait models**: Theoretical models that focus on mental, emotional, temperamental, and behavioral traits or attributes.
- **Typological models**: Theoretical models that identify broad personality types or styles.

A. Normative-Stage Models

Stages: Successive periods in development.

Normative: Events that are common for most persons.

1. Erikson: Intimacy versus Isolation
   - **Intimacy versus isolation**: According to Erikson, the sixth stage of psychosocial development, in which young adults either make commitments to others or face a possible sense of isolation and consequent self-absorption.
   - *Love:* In Erikson's theory, the virtue of the sixth stage; a mutual devotion between partners who have chosen to share their lives, have children, and help those children achieve their own healthy development.

2. Erikson's Heirs: Vaillant and Levinson
   - **Life structure**: In Levinson's theory, the underlying pattern of a person's life at a given time, built on whatever aspects of life the person finds most important.
   - *Dream:* In Levinson's theory, one's hopes about what one wishes to achieve in the future, part of the entry phase of young adulthood.

3. Evaluating Normative Stage Models
   - **Developmental tasks:** things that need to be accomplished for successful adaptation to each stage of life.

B. Timing-of-Events Model

- **Normative life events**: In the timing-of-events model, commonly expected life experiences that occur at customary times. Also called *normative age-graded events.*
- **Social clock**: Set of cultural norms or expectations for the times of life when certain important events, such as marriage, parenthood, entry into work, and retirement, should occur.

C. Trait Models: Costa and McCrae's Five Factors

Five-factor model: Theoretical model, developed and tested by Costa and McCrae, based on the "Big Five" factors underlying clusters of related personality traits: neuroticism, extraversion, openness to experience, conscientiousness, and agreeableness.

- *Neuroticism:* A cluster of six negative traits indicating emotional instability: anxiety, hostility, depression, self-consciousness, impulsiveness, and vulnerability.
- *Extraversion:* A cluster of six facets: warmth, gregariousness, assertiveness, activity, excitement-seeking, and positive emotions.
- *Open to experience:* People high in this trait are willing to try new things and embrace new ideas.
- *Conscientiousness:* People high in this trait are achievers: competent, orderly, dutiful, deliberate, and disciplined.
- *Agreeable:* People who are trusting, straightforward, altruistic, compliant, modest, and easily swayed.

1. Continuity and Change in the Five-Factor Model
2. Evaluating the Five-Factor Model

D. Typological Models
   - ***Typological approach***: An approach to personality development that looks at personality as a functioning whole that affects and reflects attitudes, values, behavior, and social interactions.
   - **Ego-resiliency**: Adaptability under potential sources of stress.
   - **Ego-control**: Self-control.
   - *Ego-resilient:* Referring to people who are well adjusted, confident, and task-focused.
   - *Overcontrolled:* Referring to people who are shy, quiet, anxious, and who withdraw from conflict.
   - *Undercontrolled:* Referring to people who are active, energetic, impulsive, stubborn, and distractible

III. FOUNDATIONS OF INTIMATE RELATIONSHIPS
Self-disclosure: Revealing important information about oneself to another.
  A. Friendship
  B. Love
   - **Triangular subtheory of love**: Sternberg's theory that patterns of love hinge on the balance among three elements: intimacy, passion, and commitment.
   - *Intimacy:* Emotional and psychological closeness to another, often including but not limited to sexual contact, and including self-disclosure.
   - *Passion:* The sexual desire component of love.
   - *Commitment:* The decision to love and stay with the beloved.

IV. NONMARITAL AND MARITAL LIFESTYLES
  A. Single Life
  B. Gay and Lesbian Relationships
  C. Cohabitation
   - **Cohabitation**: Status of a couple who live together and maintain a sexual relationship without being legally married.
    1. Types of Cohabitation: International Comparisons
      - *Consensual or informal union:* An unmarried couple living in a sexual relationship.
    2. Cohabitation in the United States
  D. Marriage
    1. What Marriage Means to Emerging and Young Adults Today
    1. Entering Matrimony
    2. Sexual Activity after Marriage
    3. Marital Satisfaction
      - Companionate Model: equalitarian marriage where couple share work and family responsibilities
      - Institutional Model: view that women are happier if they are committed to a traditional marriage
      - Equity Model: Happiness is based upon the perception of fairness.
      - Gender Model: Women are happiest in marriages characterized by gender-typical roles.
    4. Factors in Marital Success or Failure

V. PARENTHOOD

A. Parenthood as a Developmental Experience
    1. Men's and Women's Involvement in Parenthood
    2. How Parenthood Affects Marital Satisfaction
B. How Dual-Earner Families Cope
VI. WHEN MARRIAGE ENDS
A. Divorce
    1. Why Do Marriages Fail?
    2. Adjusting to Divorce
B. Remarriage and Stepparenthood

True/False Self-Test

Place a T or an F in the appropriate space. These questions are taken from the chapter content, tables, key terms, Guideposts for Study, and Checkpoints.

1. ____ Agreeableness, neuroticism, and extraversion are some of the personality traits that do not change much after age 30, according to Costa and McCrae.

2. ____ In Erikson's theory, the crisis of young adulthood is intimacy versus isolation.

3. ____ Typological research focuses on age-related social and emotional changes emerging in successive periods marked by crises.

4. ____ In Levinson's theory, transitions or crises lead to reevaluation and modification of the life structure.

5. ____ The most important message of the normative-stage models is that adults continue to change, develop, and grow.

6. ____ Young adults are marrying and having children at younger ages than did adults in the past

7. ____ Intimacy includes a sense of belonging.

8. ____ The development of identity is the crucial task of young adulthood, according to Erikson.

9. ____ People tend to be healthier physically if they have satisfying close relationships.

10. ___ Intimacy, passion, and commitment are the main components of Sternberg's triangular theory of love.

11. ___ Young adults who have conflict-filled relationship with their parents tend to leave their childhood home with the most success.

12. ___ The reasons given by young adults for remaining single include career, travel, fear of divorce, and lack of partners.

13. ___ A majority of people in the United States approve of same-sex marriage.

14. ___ Women's friendships tend to be more intimate than men's.

15. ___ Homosexual and heterosexual couples tend to be similar in the ingredients for satisfying relationships.

16. ___ The success of a marriage tends to depend upon the level of income available for the couple.

17. ___ Compared with past generations, more adults today postpone marriage or never marry.

18. ___ Gay men and lesbian women do not form enduring romantic relationships.

19. ___ Cohabitation has become common and is the norm in many countries.

20. ___ Failure to launch occurs rarely and typically welcomed by the parents since it gives more time with the adult child.

21. ___ Men benefit more than women from marriage.

22. ___ Age at marriage is a major predictor of whether a marriage will last.

23. ___ Women who give birth at a later age tend to make more money than those who give birth while young.

24. ___ Expectations and sharing of tasks can contribute to a marriage's deterioration or improvement.

25. ___ Most divorced people do not remarry, due to the stress of the divorce.

Multiple-Choice Self-Test

Circle the letter of the best answer. These questions are based on many aspects of the chapter content, in no particular order.

1. During the child-raising years, marital satisfaction typically:
a. declines.
b. increases.
c. remains unchanged.
d. greatly increases.

2. Couples who choose to remain childless do so on the basis of:
a. concern over the financial burdens of parenthood.
b. a wish to enjoy an adult lifestyle.
c. a desire to concentrate on careers.
d. All of these.

3. In the United States, the rate of divorce has risen due to:
a. women's greater financial independence.
b. parent's reluctance to expose children to parental conflict.
c. the greater "expectability" of divorce.
d. All of these.

4. Divorced men are:
a. more likely to remarry than are women.
b. not likely to remarry.
c. unusually happy.
d. just as likely to remarry as are women.

5. Who among the following is likely to adjust better to divorce?
a. older women
b. those without children
c. those with higher incomes
d. All of these.

6. A person who tends to be active, energetic, and impulsive would be described as _____ according to Block.
a. overcontrolled
b. undercontrolled
c. ego-resilient
d. ego-controlled

7. Frequency of sexual relations in a marriage:
a. declines with age.
b. increases with years of marriage.
c. is unpredictable.
d. depends entirely on religious beliefs.

8. Which of the following is a benefit of marriage?
a. Marriage meets economic needs.
b. It meets sexual and reproductive needs.
c. Marriage benefits men and women equally.
d. All of these.

9. Compared to those who marry without first living together, couples who cohabit before marriage tend to:
a. be happier.
b. have weaker marriages.
c. have stronger marriages.
d. stay together forever.

10. A major predictor of whether a marriage will last is:
a. age at marriage.
b. physical attractiveness of the partners.
c. social status of the partners.
d. job status.

11. In most cases, the burdens of a dual-earner lifestyle fall most heavily on:
a. the woman.
b. the man.
c. both the woman and the man.
d. the person with the largest income.

12. In blended families, who has the most difficulty being a stepparent?
a. stepfathers
b. stepmothers
c. both parents
d. neither parent

13. In a research study done in Israel, men whose adult attachment styles were rated as secure-autonomous also displayed:
a. poor adjustment to military training.
b. difficulty with friendships.
c. better romantic relationships.
d. poor relationships with parents.

14. According to Costa and McCrae, people who are trusting, straightforward, altruistic, compliant, modest, and easily swayed are:
a. agreeable.
b. extraverts.
c. conscientious.
d. neurotic.

15. In Levinson's model, the underlying design of a person's life is called the:
a. dream.
b. life structure.
c. mid-life transition.
d. social clock.

16. The normative-stage models of adult personality development are largely the work of:
a. George Vaillant and Daniel Levinson.
b. Sigmund Freud.
c. Albert Bandura.
d. Carl Rogers.

17. In Levinson's view, a man who is building his first provisional life structure faces these two important tasks:
a. finding a job and a home.
b. finding a wife and a home.
c. finding a dream and an occupation.
d. finding the right geographic location.

18. A characteristic of men's friendships is:
a. sharing of information and activities.
b. sharing of confidences.
c. intimacy.
d. All of these.

19. According to Sternberg, love that involves intimacy and passion, but lacks commitment is:
a. empty love.
b. romantic love.
c. fatuous love.
d. consummate love.

20. According to Sternberg, love that involves passion, but lacks intimacy and commitment is:
a. liking.
b. infatuation.
c. empty love.
d. consummate love.

21. Consummate love is:
a. easier to reach than to hold on to.
b. "love at first sight."
c. the kind of love that leads to a whirlwind courtship.
d. found in long-term relationships that lack intimacy and passion.

22. The type of love in which intimacy and commitment are both present, but in which physical attraction has died down, leaving partners close and likely to stay together is:
a. empty love.
b. companionate love.
c. consummate love.
d. liking.

23. Janice is 25 years of age. Her normative life events would likely include:
a. finding a partner.
b. completing her education and finding a job.
c. considering having a child.
d. All of these.

24. Gay and lesbian couples who live together tend to:
a. be as committed as married couples.
b. be less committed than married couples.
c. have unique commitment problems.
d. be overcommitted to each other.

25. Revealing important information about oneself to another is:
a. called disclosure.
b. part of intimacy.
c. important to forming a strong relationship.
d. All of these.

Short Essay Questions

These short essay questions are based in part on the Checkpoints in the chapter. Answer each question as completely and succinctly as possible. Check your answers by reviewing the part of the chapter that covers the Guidepost listed with each question.

1. Summarize and compare four major theoretical approaches to adult personality development. (See Guidepost 2.)

2. Summarize recent trends and gender differences in sexual attitudes and behavior. (See Guidepost 4.)

3. Identify at least three benefits of marriage. (See Guidepost 4.)

4. Compare men's and women's attitudes toward parenthood and parental responsibilities. (See Guidepost 5.)

5. Describe key factors in adjustment to divorce. (See Guidepost 6.)

Organize It!

Making lists is a fun and useful way to categorize information in your mind. After making each list, think of ways to memorize it so that you have immediate recall. Singing a list, dancing while you recite it, or simply saying it in a rhythmic pattern as you are walking, driving, or jogging allows your brain to store the information in easily retrievable form. Try it!

1. List the five factors in Costa and McCrae's trait model. (See Guidepost 2.)

    1.

    2.

    3.

    4.

    5.

2. List two factors that are important elements of intimacy. (See Guidepost 3.)

    1.

    2.

3. Discuss the three stages of the process of Recentering. (See Guidepost 1.)

    1.

    2.

    3.

4. List the four models regarding women's happiness in marriage. (See Guidepost 4.)

    1.

    2.

    3.

    4.

5. List and describe Sternberg's eight patterns of loving. (See Table 14-2 and Guidepost 3.)

    1.

    2.

    3.

    4.

    5.

    6.

    7.

    8.

Critical Thinking Questions

These questions may be used for extra credit, if your instructor agrees, or for small-group discussions.

1. Which of the models presented in this chapter seems to most adequately describe your experience of psychosocial development? Why?

2. How might our ideas of love change in the future?

3. Should homosexuals be allowed to marry? To adopt children? Be covered by a partner's health care plan?

4. Is cohabitation before marriage a good idea or a bad idea? List your reasons.

5. Should divorce be harder to obtain in the United States than it presently is? Why or why not?

Answer Keys

True/False Self-Test

1.	T	GP 2	14.	T	GP 4
2.	T	GP 2	15.	T	GP 4
3.	F	GP 2	16.	F	GP 4
4.	T	GP 2	17.	T	GP 4
5.	T	GP 2	18.	F	GP 4
6.	F	GP 4	19.	T	GP 4
7.	T	GP 3	20.	F	GP 1
8.	F	GP 2	21.	F	GP 4
9.	T	GP 3	22.	T	GP 4
10.	T	GP 3	23.	T	GP 5
11.	F	GP 1	24.	T	GP 6
12.	T	GP 4	25.	F	GP 6
13.	F	GP 4			

Multiple-Choice Self-Test

1.	a	GP 5	14.	a	GP 2
2.	d	GP 5	15.	b	GP 2
3.	d	GP 6	16.	a	GP 2
4.	a	GP 6	17.	c	GP 2
5.	d	GP 6	18.	a	GP 3
6.	b	GP 2	19.	b	GP 3
7.	a	GP 3	20.	b	GP 3
8.	d	GP 4	21.	a	GP 3
9.	b	GP 4	22.	b	GP 3
10.	a	GP 6	23.	b	GP 4
11.	a	GP 4	24.	a	GP 4
12.	b	GP 6	25.	d	GP 3
13.	c	GP 3			

PART 7: MIDDLE ADULTHOOD

CHAPTER 15: PHYSICAL AND COGNITIVE DEVELOPMENT IN MIDDLE ADULTHOOD

Chapter 15 opens Part 7 with a discussion of middle age as a cultural construct. The sensory, psychomotor, structural, systemic, sexual, and reproductive changes are discussed in the first section, along with health concerns. The second section deals with cognition, creativity, and intelligence in middle age. Education and work conclude the chapter.

Guideposts for Study

1. What are the distinguishing features of middle age?

2. What physical changes generally occur during the middle years, and what is their psychological impact?

3. What factors affect physical and mental health at midlife?

4. What cognitive gains and losses occur during middle age?

5. Do mature adults think differently than younger people do?

6. What accounts for creative achievement, and how does it change with age?

7. How are patterns of work and education changing today, and how does work contribute to cognitive development?

Detailed Chapter Outline with Key Terms

I. MIDDLE AGE: A SOCIAL CONSTRUCT
   A. When Is Middle Age?
      Middle adulthood: The years between ages 40 and 65.
   B. The Experience of Middle Age

PHYSICAL DEVELOPMENT
II. PHYSICAL CHANGES
   A. Sensory and Psychomotor Functioning
      Visual Problems Related to Age:
      - Near vision
      - Dynamic vision (reading moving signs)
      - Sensitivity to light
      - Visual search (for example, locating a sign)
      - Speed of processing
      - *Visual acuity:* sharpness of vision
      - **Presbyopia**: A lessened ability to focus on near objects due to aging.
      - **Myopia**: Nearsightedness.

- **Presbycusis**: Gradual loss of hearing, which accelerates after age 55, especially with regard to sounds at the upper frequencies.
- **Basal metabolism**: Use of energy to maintain vital functions.

B. Structural and Systemic Changes

Vital capacity: Maximum volume of air the lungs and draw in and expel and diminishes after age 40.

C. Sexuality and Reproductive Functioning
  1. Menopause and Its Meaning
     - **Menopause**: Cessation of menstruation and of ability to bear children, typically around age 50.
     - *Monopausal transition:* Gradual decrease in hormones leading to menopause.
     - **Perimenopause**: Period of several years during which a woman experiences physiological changes that bring on menopause; also called *climacteric.*
     a. Attitudes toward Menopause
     b. Symptoms and Myths
  2. Treatment of Menopausal Symptoms
  3. Changes in Male Sexuality
     - **Erectile dysfunction:** Persistent inability to achieve or maintain an erect penis for satisfactory sexual performance.
  4. Sexual Activity

III. PHYSICAL AND MENTAL HEALTH
  A. Health Trends at Midlife
     - **Hypertension**: Chronically high blood pressure.
     - **Heart Disease:** Leading cause of death for middle age.
     - **Diabetes:** Fourth cause of death in middle age.
  B. Behavioral Influences on Health
  C. Socioeconomic Status and Health
  D. Race/Ethnicity and Health
  E. Gender and Health
  1. Bone Loss and Osteoporosis
     Osteoporosis: Condition in which the bones become thin and brittle as a result of rapid calcium depletion.
  2. Breast Cancer and Mammography
     Mammography: Diagnostic x-ray examination of the breasts.
  3. Hormone Therapy
     - **Hormone therapy (HT)**: Treatment with artificial estrogen, sometimes in combination with the hormone progesterone, to relieve or prevent symptoms caused by decline in estrogen levels after menopause.
  F. Stress in Middle Age
  1. How Stress Affects Health
  2. Occupational Stress and Burnout
     - **Burnout:** prolonged response to chronic stressors in the workplace that result from a misfit between the worker and the job.
     - *Job engagement:* A persistent positive feeling of motivation and fulfillment in one's job.
  3. Unemployment Stress

G. Emotions and Health

H. Mental Health

COGNITIVE DEVELOPMENT

IV. MEASURING COGNITIVE ABILITIES IN MIDDLE AGE

    A. K. Warner Schaie: The Seattle Longitudinal Study

    B. Horn and Cattell: Fluid and Crystallized Intelligence

- **Fluid intelligence**: Type of intelligence, proposed by Horn and Cattell, which is applied to novel problems and is relatively independent of educational and cultural influences.

- **Crystallized intelligence**: Type of intelligence, proposed by Horn and Cattell, involving the ability to remember and use learned information; it is largely dependent on education and cultural background.

V. THE DISTINCTIVENESS OF ADULT COGNITION

    A. The Role of Expertise

    Encapsulation: Process of capturing fluid abilities for expert problem solving.

    C. Integrative Thought

- Integrative nature: using logic with emotion

VI. CREATIVITY

    A. Characteristics of Creative Achievers

- *Creative potential:* The talent for creativity that is present in a person, such as a child, but not yet realized in fact.

- *Creative performance:* What, and how much, a creative mind produces.

    B. Creativity and Age

VII. WORK AND EDUCATION

    A. Work versus Early Retirement

    B. Work and Cognitive Development

    C. The Mature Learner

        1. College Programs

        2. Adult Education and Work Skills

        3. Literacy Training

- **Literacy**: Ability to use printed and written information to perform in society.

True/False Self-Test

Place a T or an F in the appropriate space. These questions are taken from the chapter content, tables, key terms, Guideposts for Study, and Checkpoints.

1. _____ From young adulthood through the middle years, sensory and motor changes are small, gradual, and almost imperceptible.

2. _____ The incidences of myopia and presbyopia increase through middle age.

3. _____ By the end of middle age, one out of four people has a significant hearing loss.

4. _____ Middle-aged persons are typically in declining health, and they experience difficulty coping with stress.

5. ____ Typically, middle-aged adults are better drivers than younger ones are.

6. ____ Middle-aged workers are more likely than younger workers to suffer disabling injuries on the job.

7. ____ Heart disease becomes more common beginning in the late 40 or early 50s, especially among men.

8. ____ Some women experience menopause as early as 45.

9. ____ Sexual activity ends abruptly in midlife.

10. ____ The idea that menopause produces depression in most women is a myth.

11. ____ Men experience a gradual decline in testosterone levels and fertility as they age.

12. ____ Low income has no impact on general health in midlife.

13. ____ An accumulation of minor, everyday stressors has less impact than major life changes on physical and psychological health.

14. ____ Fluid intelligence declines earlier than crystallized intelligence.

15. ____ Postformal thought seems to be useful in situations calling for integrative thinking.

16. ____ Hot flashes have been found to be rare or infrequent among Mayan, North African, Navajo, and some Indonesian women.

17. ____ Men have an experience comparable to menopause when their levels of testosterone take a sudden drop in midlife.

18. ____ Many children of middle-aged parents are vastly ignorant of their parents' sexual activity.

19. ____ Gradual loss of bone density is an abnormal sign of aging in midlife.

20. ____ The most troublesome physical effects of menopause are linked to reduced levels of estrogen.

21. ____ The death rate for middle-aged African Americans is much lower than that of white Americans.

22. ____ Unemployment has been linked to heart attack, stroke, anxiety, and depression.

23. ____ Cognitively speaking, middle-aged people are in their prime.

24. ___ Creativity is not strongly related to intelligence.

25. ___ The recommended retirement process is to stop work completely in the late 50s and engage in recreation.

Multiple-Choice Self-Test

Circle the letter of the best answer. These questions are based on many aspects of the chapter content, in no particular order.

1. Poor health in midlife is associated with:
a. low income.
b. African American ethnicity.
c. male gender.
d. All of these.

2. Menopause increases women's susceptibility to:
a. nervous breakdowns.
b. divorce.
c. heart disease.
d. jaundice.

3. Occupational stress can be caused by:
a. work overload.
b. high pressure.
c. low control.
d. All of these.

4. Many men in midlife experience:
a. a decline in fertility.
b. more freedom in their marriages.
c. more divorce.
d. depression.

5. Sexual activity in midlife is:
a. virtually nonexistent.
b. rare.
c. diminished only slightly and gradually.
d. unchanged from early adulthood.

6. The cessation of menstruation and of ability to bear children that typically occurs at around age 50 is known as:
a. climacteric.
b. menopause.
c. perimenopause.
d. sterility.

7. A condition in which the bones become thin and brittle as a result of rapid calcium depletion is known as:
a. hypertension.
b. climacteric.
c. osteoporosis.
d. vital capacity.

8. Farsightedness associated with aging, resulting when the lens of the eye becomes less elastic, is:
a. myopia.
b. presbyopia.
c. presbycuspis.
d. HRT.

9. Adults tend to return to college primarily to:
a. improve work skills.
b. prepare for retirement.
c. enjoy life more fully.
d. become supervisors.

10. In Hoyer's terminology, progressive dedication of information processing and fluid thinking to specific knowledge systems, making knowledge more readily accessible, is known as:
a. encapsulation.
b. crystallized intelligence.
c. fluid intelligence.
d. creative performance.

11. Today the double standard of aging is:
a. waning.
b. in place.
c. escalating.
d. nonexistent.

12. Most cases of osteoporosis occur in:
a. women.
b. men.
c. adolescents.
d. young adults.

13. Bone loss can be slowed or even reversed with:
a. proper nutrition.
b. exercise.
c. quitting smoking.
d. All of these.

14. Which of the following is an effect of hormone replacement therapy?
a. It prevents bone loss.
b. It makes women more cheerful.
c. It increases fertility in midlife.
d. It causes increased sexual activity.

15. Literacy in the United States is:
a. one of the highest in the world.
b. seldom necessary for traditional women's work.
c. worse than many other industrialized countries.
d. All of these.

16. The largest single underlying factor in the excessive mortality rate for African Americans is:
a. cancer.
b. genetics.
c. poverty.
d. venereal disease.

17. The cumulative effects of stress most often show up during:
a. late adulthood.
b. adolescence.
c. middle age.
d. early adulthood.

18. Juan does not write very many poems, but nearly all of the ones he does write are very creative and good. Juan has a high:
a. level of fluid intelligence.
b. level of .crystallized intelligence
c. .myopic dysfunction.
d. quality ratio.

19. Paul is stressed at work and is experiencing emotional fatigue, cynicism, and an inability to accomplish goals. He is suffering from:
a. stress-related presbycusis.
b. sexual harassment.
c. job engagement.
d. burnout.

20. George works in a setting with people from age 18 to 75, who are all equally valued. George's work environment is:
a. age-differentiated.
b. age-integrated.
c. highly stressful.
d. highly creative.

Short Essay Questions

These short essay questions are based on the Checkpoints in the chapter. Answer each question as completely and succinctly as possible. Check your answers by reviewing the part of the chapter that covers the Guidepost listed with each question.

1. Identify and describe at least two factors that can affect women's experience of menopause. (See Guidepost 3.)

2. Summarize changes in sensory and motor functioning, as well as in body structure and systems, that may begin in middle age. (See Guidepost 2.)

3. What is the relationship between creative potential and creative performance? List several qualities of creative achievers. (See Guidepost 6.)

4. Tell how women's risks of heart disease and osteoporosis increase after menopause, and weigh the risks and benefits of hormone replacement therapy. Describe alternatives to hormone replacement therapy. (See Guidepost 3.)

5. Discuss the excessive mortality of African Americans during middle age, citing factors shown to be linked to it. (See Guidepost 3.).

Organize It!

Making lists is a fun and useful way to organize information in your mind. After making each list, think of ways to memorize it so that you have immediate recall. Singing a list, dancing while you recite it, or simply saying it in a rhythmic pattern as you are walking, driving, or jogging allows your brain to store the information in easily retrievable form. Try it!

1. List four physical changes of midlife. (See Guidepost 2.)

   1.

   2.

   3.

   4.

2. List the six basic mental abilities that showed longitudinal change in people ages 25 to 67, according to Schaie. (See Figure 15-4 and Guidepost 4.)

   1.

2.

3.

4.

5.

6.

Critical Thinking Questions

These questions can be used for extra-credit, if your instructor agrees, or in small-group discussions.

1. In your opinion, when does middle age begin? When does it end?

2. In your opinion, do middle-aged women show more concern about their appearance than middle-aged men? If so, in what ways do they show this concern?

3. What are the main sources of stress in your life?

4. If you needed surgery, would you rather go to a middle-aged doctor or a young doctor? Why?

5. In addition to those mentioned in the text, can you think of ways in which an age-integrated society would differ from an age-differentiated one?

6. Based on your own observations, do students of nontraditional age do better or worse in college than those who are younger? How do you explain your observation?

Answer Keys

True/False Self-Test

1.	T	GP 1		14. T	GP 4
2.	T	GP 2		15. T	GP 4
3.	T	GP 2		16. T	GP 3
4.	F	GP 2		17. F	GP 3
5.	T	GP 2		18. T	GP 3
6.	F	GP 3		19. F	GP 3
7.	T	GP 3		20. T	GP 3
8.	T	GP 3		21. F	GP 3
9.	F	GP 2		22. T	GP 3
10.	T	GP 3		23. T	GP 4
11.	T	GP 3		24. T	GP 6
12.	F	GP 3		25. F	GP 7
13.	F	GP 3			

Multiple-Choice Self-Test

1.	d	GP 3		11. a	GP 1
2.	c	GP 3		12. a	GP 3
3.	d	GP 3		13. d	GP 3
4.	a	GP 3		14. a	GP 3
5.	c	GP 2		15. c	GP 7
6.	b	GP 3		16. c	GP 3
7.	c	GP 3		17. c	GP 3
8.	b	GP 3		18. d	GP 6
9.	a	GP 7		19. a	GP 7
10.	a	GP 4		20. b	GP 7

CHAPTER 16: PSYCHOSOCIAL DEVELOPMENT
IN MIDDLE ADULTHOOD

This chapter explores classic theoretical approaches to midlife change, identity development, midlife crisis, and changes in relationships. Marriage, divorce, relationships with children, and aging parents are discussed in the second section. The two focus boxes discuss the possibility of a society without middle age and preventing caregiver burnout.

Guideposts for Study

1. How do developmental scientists approach the study of psychosocial development in middle adulthood?

2. What do theorists have to say about psychosocial change in middle age?

3. What issues concerning the self come to the fore during middle adulthood?

4. What role do social relationships play in the lives of middle-aged people?

5. How do marriages, cohabitations, and gay and lesbian relationships fare during the middle years, and how common is divorce at this time of life?

6. How do friendships fare during middle age?

7. How do parent-child relationships change as children approach and reach adulthood?

8. How do middle-aged people get along with parents and siblings?

9. How has grandparenthood changed, and what roles do grandparents play?

Detailed Chapter Outline with Key Terms

I. LOOKING AT THE LIFE COURSE IN MIDDLE AGE
   - Objective view: Look at trajectories and pathways.
   - Subjective view: Look at how people construct their identity and structure their lives.
II. CHANGE AT MIDLIFE: THEORETICAL APPROACHES
   Self-actualization: Full realization of human potential.
   A. Normative-Stage Models
      1. Carl G. Jung: Individuation and Transcendence
         - **Individuation**: Emergence of the true self through balancing or integration of conflicting parts of the personality.
      2. Erik Erikson: Generativity versus Stagnation
         - **Generativity versus stagnation**: The seventh critical alternative of psychosocial development, in which the middle-aged adult develops a concern with establishing, guiding, and influencing the next generation or else experiences stagnation (a sense of inactivity or lifelessness).
         - **Generativity**: Concern of mature adults for establishing, guiding, and influencing the next generation.

- *Care:* The virtue of the seventh crisis in Erikson's theory, a widening commitment to take care of the persons, the products, and the ideas one has learned to care for.
    - *a.* Generativity, Age, and Gender
    - *b.* Forms of Generativity
  3. Jung's and Erikson's Legacy: Valliant and Levinson
  Interiority: A concern with inner life (introversion or introspection), which usually appears in middle age.
  B. Timing of Events: The Social Clock
III. THE SELF AT MIDLIFE: ISSUES AND THEMES
  A. Is There a Midlife Crisis?
  - **Midlife crisis**: A supposedly stressful period triggered by review and reevaluation of one's life.
  - *Turning points:* Psychological transitions that involve significant change or transformation in the perceived meaning, purpose, or direction of a person's life.
  - **Midlife review**: Introspective examination that often occurs in middle age, leading to reappraisal and revision of values and priorities.
  - *Developmental deadlines:* Time constraints on one's ability to accomplish certain things, like having a baby.
  - *Ego-resiliency:* The ability to adapt flexibly and resourcefully to potential sources of stress.
  B. Identity Development
  1. Susan Krauss Whitbourne: Identity as a Process
     - **Identity process model**: Identity development based on processes of assimilation and accommodation.
     - **Identity assimilation**: Effort to fit new experience into an existing self-concept.
     - **Identity accommodation**: Adjusting one's identity to fit new experience.
     - **Identity balance**: Maintaining a stable sense of self while adjusting self-schemas to incorporate new information.
  2. Generativity, Identity and Age
  3. Narrative Psychology: Identity as a Life Story
     - *Narrative psychology:* Field that views the development of the self as a continuous process of constructing one's own life story.
     - *Generativity script:* Life story in which generativity plays a key role, and which gives the life story a happy ending.
     - *Redemption:* deliverance from suffering and associated with psychological well-being as part of the generativity script.
  4. Gender Identity and Gender Roles
     - **Gender crossover**: Men explore the feminine side and women explore the masculine side of roles.
  C. Psychological Well-Being and Positive Mental Health
  Positive: Referring to mental health, a sense of psychological well being and a healthy sense of self.
  1. Emotionality and Age
  2. Life Satisfaction and Age
  3. Carol Ryff: Multiple Dimensions of Well-Being

Six Dimensions of Well-Being:
- Self-acceptance
- Positive relations with others
- Autonomy
- Environmental mastery
- Purpose in life
- Personal growth
- Ethnic Conservation: Tendency to resist assimilation and cling to familiar values and practices that give meaning to life.

IV. RELATIONSHIPS AT MIDLIFE
   A. Theories of Social Contact
- **Social convoy theory**: Theory of aging, proposed by Kahn and Antonucci, which holds that people move through life surrounded by concentric circles of intimate relationships or varying degrees of closeness, on which people rely for assistance, well being, and social support.
- *Social convoys:* Circles of close friends and family members on whom people can rely for assistance, well being, and social support, and to whom they offer reciprocal care.
- **Socioemotional selectivity theory**: Theory, proposed by Carstensen, that people select social contacts throughout life on the basis of the changing relative importance of social interaction as a source of information, as an aid in developing and maintaining a self-concept, and as a source of emotional well-being.

   B. Relationships, Gender, and Quality of Life
V. CONSENSUAL RELATIONSHIPS
   A. Marriage
   B. Cohabitation
   C. Divorce
- **Marital capital**: Financial and emotional benefits built up during a long-standing marriage, which tend to hold a couple together.

   C. Marital Status, Well-Being, and Health
   D. Gay and Lesbian Relationships
VI. RELATIONSHIPS WITH MATURING CHILDREN
   A. Adolescent Children: Issues for Parents
   B. When Children Leave: The Empty Nest
- **Empty nest:** A transition that occurs when the youngest child leaves home.

   C. Parenting Grown Children
- *Tight-knit:* Intergeneration family with frequent geographical and emotional contact.
- *Sociable:* Less emotion and commitment than tight-knit.
- *Obligatory:* Interaction but little emotional attachment.
- *Detached:* Little contact, either emotional or geographical.
- *Intimate but Distant:* Little contact but retaining warm feelings.

   D. Prolonged Parenting: The "Cluttered Nest"
- Failure to launch

- **Revolving door syndrome**: Tendency for young adults to return to their parents' homes while getting on their feet or in times of financial, marital, or other trouble. (Also called the *boomerang phenomenon*.)

VII. OTHER KINSHIP TIES
  A. Relationships with Aging Parents
    1. Contact and Mutual Help
      - **Filial maturity**: Life stage when middle-aged children learn to accept and meet their parents' dependency needs.
      - **Filial crisis**: Time in which adults learn to balance love and duty to their parents with autonomy within a two-way relationship.
    2. Becoming a Caregiver for Aging Parents
    3. Strains of Caregiving
      - **Sandwich generation**: Middle-aged adults squeezed by competing needs to raise or launch children and to care for elderly parents.
      - **Caregiver burnout**: Condition of physical, mental, and emotional exhaustion affecting adults who care for aged persons.
  B. Relationships with Siblings
  C. Grandparenthood
    1. The Grandparent's Role
    2. Grandparenting after Divorce and Remarriage
    3. Raising Grandchildren
      - **Kinship care**: Care of children living without parents in the home of grandparents or other relatives, with or without a change of legal custody.

True/False Self-Test

Place a T or an F in the appropriate space. Statements are based on Guideposts for Study, tables, and chapter content.

1. ____ Developmentalists view midlife psychosocial development objectively in terms of pathways and trajectories.

2. ____ Although some theorists, such as Freud and Costa and McCrae, held that personality is essentially formed by midlife, there is growing consensus that midlife development shows change as well as stability.

3. ____ Classic theories of midlife psychosocial development include normative-crisis models and the timing-of-events model.

4. ____ Erikson's seventh psychosocial crisis is guilt versus stagnation.

5. ____ The virtue of Erikson's seventh crisis is care.

6. ____ In middle age, people no longer expect and assess their lives by the social clock.

7. ____ The "sandwich generation" is caught between competing needs to care for aging parents as well as their own children.

8. ____ Research supports the concept of a universal midlife crisis.

9. ____ Key psychosocial issues in midlife include identity development, psychological well-being, and gender identity.

10. ____ Vaillant and Levinson found no major midlife shifts in men.

11. ____ Generativity can be expressed through parenting and grandparenting.

12. ____ In midlife, identity development is no longer a central aspect according to Whitbourne.

13. ____ Much research, including Helson's longitudinal studies, suggests that for women, the fifties are a prime time of life.

14. ____ Identity style can predict adaptation to the onset of aging.

15. ____ Research generally does not support Gutmann's hypothesis of gender crossover.

16. ____ Relationships at midlife have very little effect on physical and mental health, as they did in young adulthood.

17. ____ Research on the quality of marriage suggests a decline in marital satisfaction during the childrearing years.

18. ____ Research has found that midlife is generally a period of poor mental health and declining socioeconomic status.

19. ____ According to narrative psychology, identity development is a continuous process of constructing a life story.

20. ____ Social convoys never change.

21. ____ Gay men who do not "come out" until midlife often go through a prolonged search for identity.

22. ____ During the first 20 to 24 years of marriage, couples become progressively more satisfied and happy.

23. ____ The years of marital decline are those in which parental and work responsibilities are greatest.

24. ____ Middle-aged sons are most likely to care for their aging parents.

25. ___ Women are more negatively affected by divorce at any age than are men.

Multiple-Choice Self-Test

Circle the letter of the best answer. These questions are based on many aspects of the chapter content, in no particular order.

1. The phenomenon of young adults, especially men, returning to their parents' homes, sometimes more than once, or delaying leaving the parents home, is called:
a. the sandwich generation.
b. generativity.
c. the revolving door syndrome.
d. None of these.

2. Costa and McCrae held that:
a. personality is essentially formed by midlife.
b. men and women in midlife undergo individuation.
c. people in midlife are introspective and questioning.
d. interiority is essential in midlife.

3. A normative midlife crisis is:
a. supported by research.
b. nonexistent.
c. not supported by research.
d. normal for females.

4. Compared to heterosexual couples, gay and lesbian couples tend to:
a. have more egalitarian relationships.
b. experience very few problems in balancing family and career commitment.
c. be very different in most respects.
d. None of these.

5. Carl Jung's two tasks of individuation are:
a. giving up the image of youth and acknowledging mortality.
b. leaving material wealth and growing spiritually.
c. lessening of gender differentiation and interiority.
d. None of these.

6. The individual life course is affected by:
a. interaction with others.
b. cohort and gender.
c. socioeconomic status.
d. All of these.

7. Relationships between middle-aged adults and their parents are:
a. usually distant and superficial.
b. often strained.
c. usually characterized by a strong bond of affection.
d. very competitive.

8. The "emptying of the nest" may be most stressful for:
a. mothers who have failed to prepare for the event.
b. fathers who have not been involved in childrearing.
c. Both of these.
d. Neither of these.

9. Caregiving is a source of considerable stress for:
a. everyone.
b. the sandwich generation.
c. the revolving door generation.
d. mainly people in their thirties.

10. A characteristic trait of ego-resiliency is:
a. the tendency to initiate humor.
b. emotional blandness.
c. denial of unpleasant thoughts and experiences.
d. relating to all roles in the same way.

11. The view of identity as "an organizing schema through which the individual's experiences are interpreted" is central to the theoretical model of:
a. Costa and McCrae.
b. David Elkind.
c. Susan Krauss Whitbourne.
d. Piaget.

12. Sonia is 53. Compared to when she was younger, she is likely to now have:
a. more friends.
b. fewer friends.
c. no friends.
d. a lot of acquaintances, but no close friends.

13. Gutmann's view of traditional gender roles includes the idea that:
a. gender roles evolved to ensure the security and well-being of growing children.
b. gender roles are too rigid to be useful in modern times.
c. women are stronger than men.
d. men are more vulnerable than women, emotionally speaking.

14. Circles of close friends and family members who can be relied on for assistance, well being, and social support are known as:
a. cohorts.
b. social convoys.
c. consensual relationships.
d. None of these.

15. All of the following are suggested as effective ways to prevent caregiver burnout, EXCEPT:
a. use of community support services, such as meal delivery and transportation.
b. use of respite care.
c. behavior training and/or psychotherapy.
d. pushing oneself to the edge of one's financial, emotional, and physical limits.

16. Georgia feels that she has accomplished her goals when she is working with her grandchildren and teaching them about what she considers to be important. Which of Erikson's stages is Georgia most likely in?
a. intimacy versus isolation
b. generativity versus stagnation
c. identity versus confusion
d. integrity versus despair

17. Being able to incorporate the physical changes of aging into one's identity uses:
a. identity assimilation.
b. identity accommodation.
c. identity balance.
d. all of the above are used.

18. Neugarten refers to the tendency to "explore the world within" as:
a. inferiority.
b. interiority.
c. restructuring.
d. generativity.

19. The field of psychology that views the development of the self as a process of constructing one's own life story is called:
a. narrative psychology.
b. identity process model.
c. midlife review model.
d. Timing of events psychology.

20. Who is most likely to have the role of caregiver for an elderly parent?
a. a daughter who is the only child
b. a son who is an only child
c. a daughter who lives 500 miles away from the parents with other siblings who live closer to the parents
d. a son with other siblings who lives near his aging parents

21. The field of psychology that views the development of the self as a process of constructing one's own life story is called
a. Narrative psychology.
b. Identity process model.
c. Midlife review model.
d. Timing of events model.

22. Who is most likely to have the role of caregiver to an elderly parent?
a. A daughter who is the only child.
b. A son who is the only child.
c. A daughter who lives 500 miles away with other siblings who live closer to the parent.
d. A son with other siblings who lives near his aging parents.

Short Essay Questions

These short essay questions are based on the Checkpoints in the chapter. Answer each question as completely and succinctly as possible. Check your answers by reviewing the part of the chapter that covers the Guidepost listed with each question.

1. Explain why, and under what circumstances, parents of adolescent children tend to go through a process of reappraisal or lessened well being. (See Guidepost 8.)

2. Summarize important changes that occur at midlife, according to Jung and Erikson, and tell how these ideas influenced other normative-crisis research. (See Guidepost 2.)

3. Summarize Whitbourne's model of identity, and describe ways in which people with each of the three identity styles might deal with signs of aging. (See Guidepost 3.)

4. Compare Jung's and Gutmannn's concepts of changes in gender identity at midlife, and assess the research support for each position. (See Guidepost 3.)

Organize It!

Making lists is a fun and useful way to categorize information in your mind. After making each list, think of ways to memorize it so that you have immediate recall. Singing a list, dancing while you recite it, or simply saying it in a rhythmic pattern as you are walking, driving, or jogging allows your brain to store the information in easily retrievable form. Try it!

1. List and briefly describe the five types of intergenerational relationships. (See Guidepost 7.)

    1.

    2.

    3.

    4.

    5.

2. List the 12 characteristics of ego-resilient adults. (See Guidepost 2.)

1.	7.
2.	8.
3.	9.
4.	10.
5.	11.
6.	12

3. List the five female and four male Gusii life stages. (See Windows on the World box.)

Female	*Male*
1.	1.
2.	2.
3.	3.
4.	4.
5.	

Critical Thinking Questions

These questions can be used as extra credit, if your instructor agrees, or in small-group discussions.

1. On the basis of your own observations, do you believe that adults' personalities change significantly during middle age? If so, do such changes seem to be related to maturation, or do they accompany important events, such as divorce, occupational change, or grandparenthood?

2. Did either of your parents seem to go through a midlife crisis? If you are middle-aged, did you go through a crisis? What issues, if any, made it a crisis?

3. From what you have observed, do men and women face similar or different kinds of challenges at midlife?

4. Think of a long-term married couple that you know and whom you think of as happily married. What are the characteristics of their marriage? Are they similar to those listed in the text?

5. What should be the "house rules" when adult children (with or without grandchildren) move back into their parents' home?

6. What would be the biggest challenges for you in becoming a caregiver to an aging parent or relative?

Answer Keys

True/False Self-Test

1.	T	GP 1	14.	T	GP 3
2.	T	GP 2	15.	T	GP 3
3.	T	GP 2	16.	F	GP 4
4.	F	GP 2	17.	T	GP 4
5.	T	GP 2	18.	F	GP 3
6.	F	GP 3	19.	T	GP 2
7.	T	GP 8	20.	F	GP 4
8.	F	GP 3	21.	T	GP 5
9.	T	GP 2	22.	F	GP 5
10.	F	GP 2	23.	T	GP 5
11.	T	GP 3	24.	F	GP 8
12.	F	GP 3	25.	T	GP 5
13.	T	GP 3			

Multiple-Choice Self-Test

1.	c	GP 7	11.	c	GP 3
2.	a	GP 2	12.	b	GP 4
3.	c	GP 2	13.	a	GP 3
4.	a	GP 5	14.	b	GP 4
5.	a	GP 2	15.	d	GP 8
6.	d	GP 1	16.	b	GP 2
7.	c	GP 8	17.	d	GP 3
8.	c	GP 7	18.	b	GP 2
9.	b	GP 8	19.	a	GP 2
10.	a	GP 2	20.	a	GP 8

PART 8: LATE ADULTHOOD

CHAPTER 17: PHYSICAL AND COGNITIVE DEVELOPMENT IN LATE ADULTHOOD

This chapter opens Part 8 of the text with a discussion of images of aging today, physical development, longevity, and physical and mental health in the first section. The second section explores cognitive development, including intelligence and processing abilities, memory, wisdom, and lifelong learning. The focus boxes discuss centenarians and whether "anti-aging" remedies work.

Guideposts for Study

1. How is today's older population changing?

2. How has life expectancy changed, what theories have been advanced for causes of aging, and what does research say about possibilities for extending the life span?

3. What physical changes occur during old age, and how do these changes vary among individuals?

4. What health problems are common in late adulthood, what factors influence health, and what mental and behavioral disorders so some older people experience?

5. What gains and losses in cognitive abilities tend to occur in late adulthood, and are there ways to improve older people's cognitive performance?

Detailed Chapter Outline with Key Terms

I. OLD AGE TODAY
- **Ageism**: Prejudice or discrimination against a person (most commonly an older person) based on age.
A. The Graying of the Population
B. Young Old to Oldest Old
- **Primary aging**: Gradual, inevitable process of bodily deterioration throughout the life span.
- **Secondary aging**: Aging processes that result from disease and bodily abuse and disuse and are often preventable.
- *Young Old:* People ages 65 to 74, or those who are the healthy, active majority of older adults.
- *Old Old:* People ages 75 to 84, or those who are frail, infirm, and in the minority of older people.
- *Oldest Old:* People age 85 and older
- **Functional age**: Measure of a person's ability to function effectively in his or her physical and social environment in comparison with others of the same chronological age.

- **Gerontology**: Study of the aged and the process of aging.
- **Geriatrics**: Branch of medicine concerned with processes of aging and age-related medical conditions.

PHYSICAL DEVELOPMENT

II. LONGEVITY AND AGING
- **Life expectancy**: Age to which a person in a particular cohort is statistically likely to live (given his or her current age and health status), on the basis of average longevity of a population.
- **Longevity**: Actual length of life of members of a population.
- **Life span**: The longest period that members of a species can live.
  A. Trends and Factors in Life Expectancy
    1. Gender Differences
    2. Regional and Ethnic Differences
  B. Why People Age
  Senescence: Period of the life span marked by changes in physical functioning associated with aging.
    1. Genetic-Programming Theories
       - **Genetic-programming theories**: Theories that explain biological aging as resulting from a genetically determined developmental timetable.
       - *Programmed senescence:* Theory of aging in which specific genes "switch off" before age-related losses, such as in vision or hearing, become evident.
       - *Mitochondria:* minute organisms that generate energy for cell process and are related to a possible cause of aging.
       - *Hormonal changes:* Changes in the hormones used by the body, possibly caused by genetic malfunction and creating the effects of aging.
       - *Immune system:* The body's defense system against disease.
       - *Telomeres:* The protective tips of chromosomes, which shorten each time a cell divides.
       - *Evolutional theory of aging:* A theory that states that reproductive fitness is the primary aim of natural selection and no reproductive purpose is served by putting genetic resources into life beyond the reproductive age.
    2. Variable-Rate Theories
       - **Variable-rate theories**: Theories explaining biological aging as a result of processes that vary from person to person and are influenced by both the internal and the external environment; sometimes called *error theories.*
       - **Metabolism**: Conversion of food and oxygen into energy.
       - *Wear-and-tear theory:* Theory that the body ages as a result of accumulated damage to the system beyond the body's ability to repair it.
       - *Free-radical theory:* Theory that attributes aging to the harmful effects of *free radicals*, which react with and can damage cell membranes, cell proteins, fats, carbohydrates, and even DNA.
       - **Free radicals**: Highly unstable oxygen atoms or molecules formed during metabolism.

- *Rate-of-living theory:* Theory of aging that suggests that the body can do just so much work, and the faster it works, the faster it wears out.
- *Autoimmune theory:* Theory of aging that suggests that an aging immune system can become "confused" and release antibodies that attack the body's own cells.
- **Autoimmunity**: Tendency of an aging body to mistake its own tissues for foreign invaders and to attack and destroy them.

3. How Far Can the Life Span Be Extended?
- *Prolongevity:* The concept that people can control the length and quality of their lives.
- **Survival curves**: Curves, plotted on a graph, showing percentages of a population that survive at each age level.
- **Hayflick limit**: A genetically controlled limit on the number of times a human cell will divide.

III. PHYSICAL CHANGES
  A. Organic and Systemic Changes
  Reserve capacity: Ability of body organs and systems to put forth four to ten times as much effort as usual under stress; also called *organ reserve.*
  B. The Aging Brain
   - *Neurons:* Nerve cells.
  C. Sensory and Psychomotor Functioning
   1. Vision and Hearing
      - **Cataracts**: Cloudy or opaque areas in the lens of the eye, which cause blurred vision.
      - **Age-related macular degeneration**: Condition in which the center of the retina gradually loses its ability to discern fine details; leading cause of irreversible visual impairment in older adults.
      - **Glaucoma**: Irreversible damage to the optic nerve caused by increased pressure in the eye.
   2. Strength, Endurance, Balance, and Reaction Time
  D. Sleep
   - *Insomnia:* sleeplessness.
  E. Sexual Functioning

IV. PHYSICAL AND MENTAL HEALTH
  A. Health Status
  B. Chronic Conditions and Disabilities
   1. Common Chronic Conditions
   2. Disabilities and Activity Limitations
      - **Activities of daily living (ADLs):** personal activities such as dressing, bathing, and getting around the house.
      - **Instrumental activities of daily living (IADLs):** personal activities such as shopping and attending appointments.
      - *Functional activities:* ability to do things such as walk, climb stairs, reach, lift, and carry objects.
  C. Lifestyle Influences on Health and Longevity
   1. Physical Activity
   2. Nutrition

D. Mental and Behavioral Problems
   1. Depression
   2. Dementia
   - **Dementia**: Deterioration in cognitive and behavioral functioning caused by physiological changes.
   - **Alzheimer's disease (AD)**: Progressive, degenerative brain disorder characterized by irreversible deterioration in memory, intelligence, awareness, and control of bodily functions, eventually leading to death.
   - **Parkinson's disease**: Progressive, irreversible degenerative neurological disorder, characterized by tremor, stiffness, slowed movement, and unstable posture.
   - *Multi-infarct dementia (MD):* Irreversible dementia caused by a series of small strokes.
   3. Alzheimer's Disease
       a. Symptoms
       b. Causes and Risk Factors
          - **Neurofibrillary tangles**: Twisted masses of protein fibers found in brains of persons with Alzheimer's disease.
          - **Amyloid plaque**: Waxy chunks of insoluble tissue found in the brain of persons with Alzheimer's disease.
          - **Cognitive reserve:** Similar to organ reserve—the concept that cognitive activity can strengthen the deteriorating brain and delay the onset of dementia.
       c. Diagnosis and Prediction
       d. Treatment and Prevention
          Cholinesterase inhibitors: Drugs that slow or stabilize the symptoms of Alzheimer's for at least six months to a year.

COGNITIVE DEVELOPMENT
V. ASPECTS OF COGNITIVE DEVELOPMENT
   A. Intelligence and Processing Abilities
      1. Measuring Older Adults' Intelligence
         - **Wechsler Adult Intelligence Scale (WAIS)**: Intelligence test for adults, which yields verbal and performance scores as well as a combined score.
         - *Classic aging pattern:* Tendency for scores on nonverbal performance to become lower as a person gets older, whereas verbal scores remain relatively stable.
      2. The Seattle Longitudinal Study: Use It or Lose It
      3. Everyday Problem Solving
         - Interpersonal problems: Problems related to relationships.
         - Instrumental problems: Problems related to daily events such as returning merchandise.
      4. Changes in Processing Abilities
      5. Cognitive Abilities and Mortality
   B. Memory: How Does It Change?
      1. Short-Term Memory
         - *Digit span forward:* Test of short-term memory in which a person is to repeat a sequence of numbers in the order in which the numbers were presented.
         - *Digit span backward:* Test of short-term memory in which a person is to repeat a sequence of numbers in the reverse order in which the numbers were presented.

- **Sensory memory**: Initial, brief, temporary storage of sensory information.
- **Working memory**: Short-term storage of information being actively processed.
- *Rehearsal:* Repetition of information.
- *Reorganization:* Organizing information in a way that allows better retrieval of that information.
- *Elaboration:* Mentally expanding and elaborating on information to be remembered.

2. Long-Term Memory
- **Episodic memory**: Long-term memory of specific experiences or events, linked to time and place.
- **Semantic memory**: Long-term memory of general factual knowledge, social customs, and language.
- **Procedural memory**: Long-term memory of motor skills, habits, and ways of doing things, which can often be recalled without conscious effort; sometimes called *implicit memory.*

3. Speech and Memory: Effects of Aging
- Verbal retrieval: Inability to retrieve information such as the tip-of-the-tongue experience.

4. Why Do Some Memory Systems Decline?
    a. Neurological Change
    b. Problems in Encoding, Storage, and Retrieval
    - Storage: capacity to hold information.
    - Retrieval system: ability to recall or recognize information that has been stored.

C. Wisdom
- *Transcendence*: Detachment from preoccupation with self.

True/False Self-Test

Place a T or an F in the appropriate space. These questions are taken from the chapter content, tables, key terms, Guideposts for Study, and Checkpoints.

1. _____ According to studies using Metamemory in Adulthood, older adults may overestimate their memory loss, perhaps because of stereotypes of aging memory.

2. _____ According to Baltes's study of wisdom, older adults show it as much or more than younger adults.

3. _____ Lifelong learning serves mainly as entertainment for older adults.

4. _____ Although the effects of primary aging may be beyond people's control, they can often avoid the effects of secondary aging.

5. _____ Specialists in gerontology refer to people 85 and older as "old."

6. _____ Survival curves do not support the idea of a definite limit to the human life span.

7. ____ Heart disease, cancer, and stroke are the three leading causes of death for people older than 65.

8. ____ White people tend to have greater longevity than do black people.

9. ____ Men tend to have a greater life expectancy than women.

10. ___ The brain seems to be able to grow new neurons and build new connections late in life.

11. ___ A common vision disorder for the elderly is macular degeneration.

12. ___ Major depressive disorder tends to be underdiagnosed in older adults.

13. ___ Crystallized intelligence increases into old age.

14. ___ The Seattle Longitudinal Study found that cognitive functioning in late adulthood is highly variable.

15. ___ The ability to solve interpersonal and emotionally charged problems declines sharply in late life.

16. ___ The Hayflick limit has established that cells can continue to divide an unlimited number of times.

17. ___ Persons over age 65 tend to sleep more and dream more than when they were younger.

18. ___ Many simple changes in the household can help reduce accidents and falls for an elderly person.

19. ___ Depression, alcoholism, and Alzheimer's disease can all be reversed with treatment.

20. ___ According to Baltes, the pragmatics of intelligence tends to decline rapidly in old age.

Multiple-Choice Self-Test

Circle the letter of the best answer. These questions are based on many aspects of the chapter content, in no particular order.

1. The graying of the population is largely due to:
   a. high birth rates in the mid-20th century.
   b. high immigration rates in the mid-20th century.
   c. Neither of these.
   d. Both of these.

2. Leonard Hayflick found that:
   a. human cells in the laboratory will divide no more than 50 times.
   b. mouse genes will combine with human genes.
   c. the onset of senescence is highly predictable.
   d. None of these.

3. Free-radical theory is an example of which kind of theory?
   a. genetic-programming theory
   b. variable-rate theory
   c. operant conditioning
   d. survival curve theory

4. Genetic-programming theory implies:
   a. the Yalta limit.
   b. a genetically decreed maximum to the life span.
   c. that there is no limit to the life span.
   d. that life span can be expanded by cloning.

5. The theories that explain biological aging as a result of processes that vary from person to person and are influenced by both the internal and external environment are:
   a. biological theories.
   b. free-radical theories.
   c. autoimmune theories.
   d. variable-rate theories.

6. Telomeres are:
   a. hormones that control aging.
   b. the protective tips of chromosomes.
   c. highly unstable atoms formed during metabolism.
   d. random bits of RNA.

7. The theory that proposes that specific genes may "switch off" before age-related changes become evident is:
   a. immunological theory.
   b. free-radical theory.
   c. programmed senescence theory.
   d. endocrine theory.

8. Free-radical theory focuses on:
   a. the harmful effects of free radicals.
   b. the beneficial effects of free radicals.
   c. the beneficial effects of oxygen.
   d. None of these.

9. Recent data on centenarians seems to:
   a. contradict the view that the upper limit for human life span is 110 to 120 years.
   b. supports the idea of the running out of the cellular clock.
   c. support the Hayflick limit.
   d. None of these.

10. Dietary restriction theories support the view that:
    a. diet has no effect on aging.
    b. rate of metabolism is a crucial determinant of aging.
    c. caloric restriction increases the production of free radicals.
    d. dietary restriction weakens the immune system.

11. Marcella has a cloudy covering on the lenses of her eyes that restrict her vision. She is likely to be diagnosed with:
a. macular degeneration.
b. cataracts.
c. glaucoma.
d. telomeres.

12. Cataracts occur in:
a. more than half of people older than 65.
b. very few people older than 65.
c. only persons who spend too much time in the sun.
d. females, mainly.

13. The most prominent early symptom of Alzheimer's disease is:
a. inability to use language.
b. failure to recognize family members.
c. inability to recall recent events or take in new information.
d. inability to eat without help.

14. Which of the following is NOT a symptom of Alzheimer's disease?
a. misplacing everyday items
b. forgetting simple words
c. rapid, dramatic mood swings and personality changes; loss of initiative
d. getting lost on one's own block

15. The diagnosis of Alzheimer's disease in a living person is:
a. about 85% accurate.
b. made on the basis of physical tests.
c. made on the basis of neurological tests.
d. All of these.

16. Symptoms of depression are:
a. diagnosed too infrequently in late life.
b. less common in older adults than in younger ones.
c. a natural part of aging.
d. a sign of weakness.

17. Cognitive deterioration is:
a. inevitable.
b. irreversible.
c. related to disuse.
d. overestimated.

18. The Metamemory in Adulthood questionnaire looks at:
a. beliefs about one's own memory.
b. selection of strategies for remembering.
c. use of strategies for remembering.
d. All of these.

19. Who is likely to have the greatest life expectancy?
a. an African American woman
b. an African American man
c. a white woman
d. a white man

20. Eighty-year-old Christine is an excellent *Trivial Pursuit* player because she knows so much about history and cultural events. She is better than her teenage grandchildren because of an increase in _____ intelligence.
a. fluid
b. crystallized
c. dual process
d. sensory memory

Short Essay Questions

These short essay questions are based in part on the Checkpoints in the chapter. Answer each question as completely and succinctly as possible. Check your answers by reviewing the part of the chapter that covers the Guidepost listed with each question.

1. Give examples of negative and positive stereotypes about aging. (See Guidepost 1.)

2. Compare and contrast two kinds of theories of biological aging, their implications, and supporting evidence. (See Guidepost 2.)

3. Give several reasons why older adults' intelligence tends to be underestimated. (See Guidepost 4.).

4. Summarize the findings of the Seattle Longitudinal Study with regard to cognitive changes in old age. (See Guidepost 5.)

Organize It!

Making lists is a fun and useful way to categorize information in your mind. After making each list, think of ways to memorize it so that you have immediate recall. Singing a list, dancing while you recite it, or simply saying it in a rhythmic pattern as you are walking, driving, or jogging allows your brain to store the information in easily retrievable form. Try it!

1. List three main causes of dementia in older adults. (See Guidepost 4.)

    1.

    2.

    3.

2. List four stereotypes that are misconceptions about aging. (See Guidepost 1.)

    1.

    2.

    3.

    4.

3. List four aspects of memory that appear nearly as efficient in older adults as in younger people. (See Guidepost 5.)

    1.

    2.

    3.

    4.

Critical Thinking Questions

These questions can be used for extra-credit, if your instructor agrees, or in small-group discussions.

1. What stereotypes about aging have you seen or heard in the media or in everyday life?

2. If it were possible, would you want to live forever?

3. If you could live as long as you wanted to, how long would you choose to live?

4. What are some ways you might try to maintain your cognitive abilities, such as memory and problem solving, well into old age?

Answer Keys

True/False Self-Test

1.	T	GP 1		11.	T	GP 3
2.	T	GP 5		12.	T	GP 4
3.	F	GP 5		13.	T	GP 5
4.	T	GP 2		14.	T	GP 5
5.	F	GP 1		15.	F	GP 5
6.	F	GP 2		16.	F	GP 2
7.	T	GP 2		17.	F	GP 3
8.	T	GP 2		18.	T	GP 3
9.	F	GP 2		19.	F	GP 4
10.	T	GP 3		20.	F	GP 5

Multiple-Choice Self-Test

1.	d	GP 1		11.	b	GP 3
2.	a	GP 2		12.	a	GP 3
3.	b	GP 2		13.	c	GP 4
4.	b	GP 2		14.	a	GP 4
5.	d	GP 2		15.	d	GP 4
6.	b	GP 2		16.	a	GP 4
7.	c	GP 2		17.	c	GP 5
8.	a	GP 2		18.	d	GP 7
9.	a	GP 2		19.	c	GP 1
10.	b	GP 2		20.	b	GP 4

CHAPTER 18: PSYCHOSOCIAL DEVELOPMENT
IN LATE ADULTHOOD

This chapter explores the stability of personality traits, normative issues and tasks, and coping models of "successful aging," as well as personal and consensual relationships in late life. The final section of the chapter deals with nonmarital kinship ties. The two focus boxes examine the question of whether longevity and health may be related to personality and a glimpse of aging in Japan.

Guideposts for Study

1. Does personality change in old age, and what special issues and tasks do older people need to deal with?

2. What strategies and resources contribute to older adults' well-being and mental health?

3. How do older adults handle work and retirement decisions, financial resources and living arrangements?

4. How do personal relationships change in old age, and what is their effect on well-being?

5. What are the characteristics of long-term marriages in late life, and what impact do widowhood, divorce, and remarriage, have at this time?

6. How do unmarried older people and those in cohabiting and gay and lesbian relationships fare, and how does friendship change in old age?

7. How do older adults get along with—or without—grown children and with siblings, and how do they adjust to great-grandparenthood?

Detailed Chapter Outline with Key Terms

I. THEORY AND RESEARCH ON PSYCHOSOCIAL DEVELOPMENT
   A. Erik Erikson: Normative Issues and Tasks
      - **Ego integrity versus despair**: According to Erikson, the eighth and final critical crisis of psychosocial development, in which people in late adulthood either achieve a sense of integrity of the self by accepting the lives they have lived, and thus accept death, or yield to despair that their lives cannot be relived.
      - *Wisdom:* The virtue in Erikson's eighth stage, an informed and detached concern with life in the face of death.
   B. The Five-Factor Model: Personality Traits in Old Age
      1. Measuring Stability and Change in Personality
         - *Average Levels:* Measurement of typical traits in a population.
         - *Within Individuals:* Measurement of change within the individual person.
         - *Rank-order Comparisons:* Measurement of different persons on a given trait.
      2. Personality, Emotionality, and Well-Being

- Negative emotions such as restlessness, boredom, loneliness, unhappiness, and depression, decrease with age.
- Positive emotions, excitement, interest, pride and sense of accomplishment remain stable; decrease only slightly in late life.
- *Extraverted:* Outgoing and socially oriented personality.
- *Neurotic:* Moody, touchy, anxious, and restless personality.
- *Conscientiousness:* Dependability

II. WELL-BEING IN LATE ADULTHOOD
  A. Coping and Mental Health
   - **Coping**: Adaptive thinking or behavior aimed at reducing or relieving stress that arises from harmful, threatening, or challenging conditions.
   1. George Vaillant: Adaptive Defenses
     - *Adaptive defenses:* Mature defenses, in Vaillant's theory, such as altruism, humor, suppression, anticipation, and sublimation.
   2. Cognitive-Appraisal Model
     - **Cognitive-appraisal model**: Model of coping, proposed by Lazarus and Folkman, which holds that, on the basis of continuous appraisal of their relationship with the environment, people choose appropriate coping strategies to deal with situations that tax their normal resources.
     a. Coping Strategies: Problem-focused versus Emotion-focused
        - **Problem-focused coping**: In the cognitive-appraisal model, coping strategy directed toward eliminating, managing, or improving a stressful situation.
        - **Emotion-focused coping**: In the cognitive-appraisal model, coping strategy directed toward managing the emotional response to a stressful situation to lessen its physical or psychological impact.
   3. Age Differences in Choice of Coping Styles
     a. *Proactive coping:* Confronting or expressing one's emotions or seeking social support.
     b. *Passive coping:* Avoidance, denial, or suppression of emotions or acceptance of the situation as it is.
     c. **Ambiguous loss**: A loss that is not clearly defined or does not bring closure.
   3. Does Religion or Spirituality Affect Health and Well-Being?
  B. Models of "Successful" or "Optimal" Aging
   - Successful or Optimal Aging: When people experience late adulthood as a positive stage of life, feeling healthy, competent, and in control of their lives.
   1. Disengagement Theory versus Activity Theory
     - **Disengagement theory**: Theory of aging, proposed by Cumming and Henry, which holds that successful aging is characterized by mutual withdrawal between the older person and society.
     - **Activity theory**: Theory of aging, proposed by Neugarten and others, which holds that, in order to age successfully, a person must remain as active as possible.
   2. Continuity Theory
   - **Continuity Theory**: Theory of aging, described by Atchley, which holds that in order to age successfully people must maintain a balance of continuity and change in both the internal and external structures of their lives.

3. The Role of Productivity
4. Selective Optimization with Compensation
- *Selective optimization with compensation (SOC):* In Baltes's dual-process model, strategy for maintaining or enhancing overall cognitive functioning by using stronger abilities to compensate for those that have weakened.
- *Selecting:* Person conserves energy by selecting fewer activities
- *Optimizing:* Making the most of the person's resources.
- *Compensating for Losses:* Develop alternative ways to achieve goals.

III. PRACTICAL AND SOCIAL ISSUES RELATED TO AGING
   A. Work and Retirement
      1. Trends in Late-Life Work and Retirement
      2. How Does Age Affect Attitudes toward Work and Job Performance?
      3. Life after Retirement
- **Family-focused lifestyle**: Pattern of retirement activity that revolves around family, home, and companions.
- **Balanced investment**: Pattern of retirement activity allocated among family, work, and leisure.
- **Serious leisure**: Leisure activity requiring skill, attention, and commitment.

   B. How Do Older Adults Fare Financially?
   C. Living Arrangements
      1. Aging in Place
      2. Living Alone
      3. Living with Adult Children
      4. Living in Institutions
      5. Alternative Housing Options
- *Assisted living:* Living in a facility that enables the older person to maintain privacy, dignity, autonomy, and a sense of control over their own homelike space, while giving them easy access to needed personal and health care services.

IV. PERSONAL RELATIONSHIPS IN LATE LIFE
   A. Theories of Social Contact and Social Support
- *Social convoy theory:* Theory of aging proposed by Kahn and Antonucci, which holds that people move through life surrounded by concentric circles of intimate relationships or varying degrees of closeness, on which people rely for assistance, well-being, and social support.
- *Socioemotional selectivity theory:* Theory proposed by Carstensen that people select social contacts throughout life on the basis of the changing relative importance of social interaction as a source of information, as an aid in developing and maintaining a self-concept, and as a source of emotional well-being.

   B. The Importance of Social Relationships
   C. The Multigenerational Family
- *Lineal:* Family style in which the emphasis is on intergenerational obligations, with power and authority lodged in the older generation.
- *Collateral:* Family style in which the emphasis is on egalitarian relationships, with flexible household structures.

V. MARITAL RELATIONSHIPS

A. Long-Term Marriage
B. Widowhood
C. Divorce and Remarriage
D. Single Life
E. Cohabitation
F. Gay and Lesbian Relationships
    Status: A characteristic of the self.
G. Friendships
VI. NONMARITAL KINSHIP TIES
A. Relationships with Adult Children
B. Relationships with Siblings
C. Becoming Great-Grandparents

True-False Self-Test

Place a T or an F in the appropriate space. These questions are taken from the chapter content, tables, key terms, Guideposts for Study, and Checkpoints.

1. ___ According to Erikson, the crowning achievement of late adulthood is a sense of ego integrity.

2. ___ Wisdom, according to Erikson, is accepting with no regrets the life one has lived.

3. ___ According to Erikson, people who do not have acceptance are overwhelmed by despair.

4. ___ According to Vaillant's research, people in old age continue to adapt, much as they have adapted throughout their lives.

5. ___ Problem-focused coping focuses on eliminating, managing, or improving a stressful condition.

6. ___ One problem-focused strategy is to divert attention away from the problem.

7. ___ Apparently, with age, people develop less flexible coping strategies.

8. ___ Religion is an important source of emotion-focused coping for many older adults.

9. ___ Older adults have a more difficult time regulating their emotions than do younger people.

10. ___ Elderly white people are more involved with religious activity than are older African Americans.

11. ___ Religious involvement has a mostly positive impact on physical and mental health and longevity.

12. ____ Most older Americans prefer to "age in place."

13. ____ Researchers disagree on how to define and measure "successful aging."

14. ____ According to disengagement theory, aging normally brings a gradual reduction in social involvement and greater preoccupation with the self.

15. ____ Isolation in late adulthood is healthy since it reduces the risk of catching any illnesses.

16. ____ Disengagement theory has received widespread research support.

17. ____ Children of aging parents have the obligation to make medical and relational decisions for their parents.

18. ____ Older adults typically have friendships that focus on companionship and support.

19. ____ A never-married woman is more likely to be lonely in late adulthood than women who were married and are divorced or widowed.

20. ____ Older people tend to spend more time with friends than with family and friends tend to become the primary emotional support.

Multiple-Choice Self-Test

Circle the letter of the best answer. These questions are based on many aspects of the chapter content, in no particular order.

1. In the United States, the number of people older than 65 years of age who live in institutions is:
   a. a small percentage.
   b. growing steadily.
   c. about 50 percent.
   d. about 75%.

2. Older adults tend to:
   a. grow more depressed.
   b. have more negative emotions.
   c. grow more content and satisfied with life.
   d. None of these.

3. The retirement pattern that consists of spending time engaged in playing chess at a competitive level is:
   a. family-focused.
   b. balanced investment.
   c. serious leisure.
   d. All of these.

4. The person least likely to be lonely in old age is:
   a. a person who never married.
   b. a widow.
   c. a widower.
   d. a divorced person.

5. According to social convoy theory, changes in social contact typically affect:
   a. selectivity about friendships.
   b. the chances of marriage.
   c. a person's outer, less intimate social circles.
   d. emotional needs.

6. In multigenerational families, Hispanic and Asian American cultures traditionally emphasize:
   a. collateral, egalitarian relationships.
   b. lineal, intergenerational obligations.
   c. highly flexible household structures.
   d. None of these.

7. Marriage in late life is:
   a. more common for men than for women.
   b. more common for older black men than for white men.
   c. Rare for all ethnic and racial groups.
   d. less likely to succeed than marriage in early adulthood.

8. Older, never-married people are:
   a. more likely than older divorced or widowed people to prefer single life.
   b. less likely to be lonely.
   c. a small percentage of the U.S. population.
   d. All of these.

9. Compared to those with more distant relationships, older people who are close to their sisters:
   a. feel better about life and worry less about aging.
   b. feel more anxiety and worry more about aging.
   c. are not different from those who have no siblings.
   d. are not as satisfied as those who are close to their brothers.

10. By old age, conflict and overt sibling rivalry tend to:
a. decrease.
b. increase.
c. remain unchanged.
d. be the most common among brothers.

11. Mario, age 92, has stopped taking his medications and remains in his bed without engaging with others. There would be concern about what mental health issue?
a. depression
b. self-neglect
c. dementia
d. physical abuse

12. Margaret lives in a setting with other elderly persons and has her own apartment. Staff members provide some help with bathing and dressing and meals and transportation is provided. This is an example of what type of living arrangement?
a. foster-care home
b. assisted-living facility
c. nursing home
d. All of these.

13. Joseph and Justine are getting married in their 70s. Compared with younger persons, their marriage is more likely to be characterized by:
a. less trust and more jealousy.
b. greater trust and acceptance.
c. increased passion.
d. deep sharing of personal feelings.

14. Women are more likely than men to:
a. remarry if widowed.
b. remain single if widowed.
c. report greater happiness with a marriage in late adulthood
d. have greater marital satisfaction.

15. A major issue for gay and lesbian couples in late adulthood is:
a. lack of access to a partner's Social Security benefits.
b. discrimination in nursing homes.
c. insensitive policies by hospitals and social agencies.
d. All of these.

Short Essay Questions

These short essay questions are based on the Checkpoints in the chapter. Answer each question as completely and succinctly as possible. Check your answers by reviewing the part of the chapter that covers the Guidepost listed with each question.

1. Compare two ways in which researchers try to measure successful or optimal aging, and point out the advantages and drawbacks of each method. (See Guidepost 2.)

2. Compare and contrast disengagement theory, activity theory, continuity theory, and productive aging. (See Guidepost 2.)

3. Identify several values that great-grandparents find in their role. (See Guidepost 7.)

Organize It!

Making lists is a fun and useful way to categorize information in your mind. After making each list, think of ways to memorize it so that you have immediate recall. Singing a list, dancing while you recite it, or simply saying it in a rhythmic pattern as you are walking, driving, or jogging allows your brain to store the information in easily retrievable form. Try it!

1. List the components of successful aging. (See Guidepost 2.)

    1.

    2.

    3.

2. List the eight forms of group living arrangements suggested for older adults. (See Table 18-1 and Guidepost 3.)

    1.

    2.

    3.

    4.

    5.

    6.

    7.

    8.

3. List 5 of the 18 United Nations Principles for Older Persons. (See Table 18-2 and Guidepost 6.)

    1.

    2.

    3.

    4.

    5.

4. List and describe the six types of maltreatment of the elderly. (See Box 18-2.)

    1.

    2.

    3.

    4.

    5.

    6.

Critical Thinking Questions

These questions can be used as extra-credit, if your instructor agrees, or in small-group discussions.

1. Which type of coping do you think you tend to use more: problem-focused coping or emotion-focused coping? What type of coping do your parents use? Your grandparents? In what kinds of situations does each type seem most efficient?

2. What is your definition of successful aging?

3. When do you expect to retire (if ever), and what do you want to do when you are retired?

4. If you were to become unable to care for yourself when old, what type of living arrangement would you want to have?

Answer Keys

True/False Self-Test

1.	T	GP 1		11.	T	GP 2
2.	T	GP 1		12.	T	GP 3
3.	T	GP 1		13.	T	GP 3
4.	T	GP 2		14.	T	GP 3
5.	T	GP 2		15.	F	GP 3
6.	F	GP 2		16.	F	GP 3
7.	F	GP 2		17.	F	GP 7
8.	F	GP 2		18.	T	GP 6
9.	F	GP 2		19.	F	GP 5
10.	F	GP 2		20.	F	GP 6

Multiple-Choice Self-Test

1.	a	GP 1		9.	a	GP 7
2.	c	GP 2		10.	a	GP 7
3.	c	GP 3		11.	a	GP 2
4.	a	GP 6		12.	b	GP 3
5.	c	GP 4		13.	b	GP 5
6.	b	GP 3		14.	b	GP 5
7.	a	GP 5		15.	D	GP 6
8.	d	GP 5				

PART 9: THE END OF LIFE

CHAPTER 19: DEALING WITH DEATH AND BEREAVEMENT

This chapter looks at the issues we all face as we approach the end of life. Some of the topics covered in this chapter are care of the dying, grief patterns, dealing with death at every stage of the life span, special losses such as those of a child or parent, suicide and assisted suicide, and finding meaning and purpose in life and death. The focus boxes discuss ambiguous loss and the gift of organ donations.

Guideposts for Study

1. How do attitudes and customs concerning death differ across cultures, and what are the implications of the "mortality revolution" in developed countries?

2. How do people deal with their own dying, and how do they grieve a loss?

3. What special challenges are involved in surviving a spouse, a parent, or a child, or in mourning a miscarriage?

4. Why are attitudes toward hastening death changing, and what concerns do these practices raise?

5. How can people overcome fear of dying and come to terms with death?

Detailed Chapter Outline with Key Terms

I. CHANGING MEANINGS OF DEATH AND DYING
   A. The Cultural Context
   - *Biological Death:* Physical end of life.
   - *Social Aspects of Death:* Change in roles and status due to death.
   - *Cultural Aspects of Death:* Variations on the ways cultures view death.
   - *Historical Aspects of Death:* Changes in the way persons view death over time.
   - *Legal Aspects of Death:* Death and law in a society.
   - *Psychological Aspects of Death:* Emotional views of death and the process of dying and grieving.
   - *Developmental Aspects of Death:* Different views of death due to development from child to adult.
   - *Medical Aspects of Death:* Physicians and other medical providers view of death.
   - *Ethical Aspects of Death:* The dilemmas facing a society about when and how death occurs.
   A. The Cultural Context
   - *Shiva:* Jewish custom in which mourners vent their feelings and share memories of the deceased.
   - *Mummification:* Early form of embalming to preserve a body so the soul can return to it.
   B. The Mortality Revolution

- **Thanatology**: Study of death and dying.
  C. Care of the Dying
- **Hospice care**: Warm, personal, patient- and family-centered care for a person with a terminal illness.
- **Palliative care**: Care aimed at relieving pain and suffering and allowing the terminally ill to die in peace, comfort, and dignity.
II. FACING DEATH AND LOSS
  A. Physical and Cognitive Changes Preceding Death
- **Terminal Drop:** Decline in cognitive abilities shortly before death, also called terminal decline.
  B. Confronting One's Own Death
  Kübler-Ross's Five Stages of Coming to Terms with Death:
    1. Denial (refusal to accept the reality of what is happening)
    2. Anger
    3. Bargaining for extra time
    4. Depression
    5. Acceptance
  C. Patterns of Grieving
- **Bereavement**: The change in status and roles due to a death and may include social and economic consequences.
- **Grief**: Emotional response experienced in the early phases of bereavement.
  D. The Classic Grief Work Model
- **Grief work**: Common pattern of working out psychological issues connected with grief, in which the bereaved person accepts the loss, releases the bond with the deceased, and rebuilds a life without that person.
- *The Three Stages of Grief Work:*
    1. Shock and disbelief: Period immediately after the death where survivors often feel lost and confused.
    2. Preoccupation with the memory of the dead person: Second stage that can be two years in length where a person attempts to come to terms with the death but cannot yet accept the death.
    3. Resolution: The final stage of grief when the person renews interest in everyday activities.
  E. Grieving: Multiple Variations
- Resilience: a low and gradually diminishing level of distress.
- Three patterns of grieving
- *Ambiguous loss:* Referring to a death that is unclear, such as a report of someone missing in action and presumed dead.
  F. Attitudes about Death and Dying Across the Life Span
    1. Childhood and Adolescence
- *Irreversible:* Child's understanding that death is permanent and cannot be undone.
- *Universal and inevitable:* Child's understanding that all living things must die.
- *Nonfunctional:* Child's understanding that all life functions end at death.
    2. Adulthood
III. SIGNIFICANT LOSSES
  A. Surviving a Spouse

B. Losing a Parent in Adulthood
C. Losing a Child
D. Mourning a Miscarriage
- *Mizuko kuyo:* Buddhist rite of apology and remembrance for miscarried children (*mizuko* means "water child," the Japanese word for a miscarried child).

IV. MEDICAL, LEGAL, AND ETHICAL ISSUES: THE "RIGHT TO DIE"
A. Suicide
- *Suicide Attempts:* trying but not completing suicide.
B. Hastening Death
- **Passive euthanasia**: Deliberate withholding or discontinuation of life-prolonging treatment of a terminally ill person in order to end suffering or allow death with dignity.
- **Active euthanasia**: Deliberate action taken to shorten the life of a terminally ill person in order to end suffering or to allow the death with dignity; also called *mercy killing.*
- *Voluntary:* In referring to euthanasia, whether it is done at the direct request or to carry out the expressed wishes of the person whose death results.
1. Advance Directives
   - **Advance directive ("living will")**: Document specifying the type of care wanted by the will maker in the event of terminal illness.
   - **Durable power of attorney**: Legal instrument that appoints an individual to make decisions in the event of another person's incapacitation.
   - *Medical durable power of attorney:* Legal instrument that appoints an individual to make decisions about health care in the event of another person's incapacitation.
2. Assisted Suicide: Pros and Cons
   Assisted Suicide: A physician or someone else helps bring about a self-inflicted death.
   - Ethical arguments for: Based on the principles of autonomy and self-determination and that mentally competent persons have rights to control the quality, timing, and nature of their death.
   - Legal arguments for: Based upon regulation of practices that already occur.
   - Ethical arguments against: Based upon view that taking a life is wrong and concern about protection of disadvantaged.
   - Medical arguments against: Based upon possibility of misdiagnosis, likelihood of future treatments, incorrect prognosis, and belief that helping someone die is incompatible with physician's role.
   - Legal arguments against: Based on enforceability of safeguards and lawsuits when family members disagree.
3. Legalizing Physician Aid in Dying
4. End-of-Life Options and Cultural Attitudes
5. End-of-Life Options and Diversity Concerns

V. FINDING MEANING AND PURPOSE IN LIFE AND DEATH
A. Reviewing a Life
   Life review: Reminiscence about one's life in order to see its significance.
B. Development: A Lifelong Process

True/False Self-Test

Place a T or and F in the appropriate space. Statements are based on Guideposts for Study, tables, and other chapter content.

1. ____ Death and loss are universal experiences and have no cultural context.

2. ____ Disposal of the body varies due to culture and religion.

3. ____ The three leading causes of death are heart disease, cancer, and strokes.

4. ____ The focus of hospice care is on preventing death.

5. ____ Kübler-Ross outlined five stages in coming to terms with death.

6. ____ Grief work is the typical pattern of three stages of dealing with loss.

7. ____ The second stage of grief work is shock and disbelief.

8. ____ Not all people who suffer a loss show signs of depression.

9. ____ Children understand that death is irreversible by age 3.

10. ____ People who feel that their lives have been meaningful may be better able to face death.

11. ____ Widowhood is the same for men as it is for women.

12. ____ The death of a second parent is usually not as painful as the death of the first parent.

13. ____ Suicide rates began declining in the late 1990s.

14. ____ Passive euthanasia is also known as mercy killing.

15. ____ Advance directives help many patients in comas or persistent vegetative states.

16. ____ In the United States, assisted suicide is illegal in almost all states.

17. ____ As the population ages, the issue of aid in dying will become more pressing.

18. ____ A life review is a process of reminiscence that helps a person see the importance of his or her life.

19. ____ Dying can be a developmental experience.

20. ____ Those who recall mostly negative events during the life review develop ego integrity.

Multiple-Choice Self-Test

Circle the letter of the best answer. These questions are based on many aspects of the chapter content.

1. Customs regarding disposal and remembrance of the dead are:
   a. universal and unchanging.
   b. different from culture to culture.
   c. always governed by secular laws.
   d. None of these.

2. Today's practice of embalming developed from the ancient practice of:
   a. sitting shiva.
   b. premature burial.
   c. mummification.
   d. cremation.

3. 3. In the 1900s, the top causes of death in the United States were:
   a. diseases that affected mostly elderly people.
   b. heart disease, cancer, and strokes.
   c. diseases that affected mostly middle-aged people.
   d. diseases that affected mostly children and young adults.

4. Care that focuses on relief of pain and suffering and allowing the person to die with dignity is known as:
   a. palliative care.
   b. hospital care.
   c. terminal care.
   d. thanatos care.

5. In the _____ stage of coming to terms with death, according to Kübler-Ross, a person refuses to accept the reality of what is happening.
   a. denial
   b. anger
   c. bargaining
   d. depression

6. The last stage of coming to terms with death, according to Kübler-Ross, is:
   a. anger.
   b. acceptance.
   c. bargaining.
   d. depression.

7. The emotional response experienced during the early phases after loss of a loved one is called:
   a. bereavement.
   b. grief work.
   c. grief.
   d. shock.

8. When memories of the dead person bring fond feelings mingled with sadness, the person is said to have reached the _____ stage of grief work.
   a. first
   b. second
   c. third
   d. fourth

9. Acceptance of a loved one's death may be particularly difficult if the loss is:
   a. ambiguous.
   b. sudden.
   c. slow and drawn out.
   d. unexpected.

10. Which of the following is NOT one of the concepts about death that children reach at about the age of 5 or 7?
    a. Death is irreversible.
    b. Death is universal.
    c. A dead person is nonfunctional.
    d. They, themselves, will not die.

11. Which of the following may make a loss more difficult for a child?
a. The child had a troubled relationship with the person who died.
b. The surviving parent depends too much on the child.
c. The death was unexpected.
d. All of these.

12. When they reach ___ ___, people realize more keenly than before that they are going to die.
a. young adulthood
b. middle age
c. late adulthood
d. adolescence

13. Which of the following is TRUE concerning widowhood?
a. Men are more likely to be widowed than women.
b. Women tend to be widowed at an older age than are men.
c. One-third of women lose their husbands by age 65.
d. One-third of men lose their wives by age 65.

14. The death of a parent for an adult child can:
a. be a maturing experience.
b. bring changes in other relationships.
c. free an adult child to spend more time and energy on other relationships.
d. All of these.

15. The loss of a child may draw couples closer together if:
a. the marriage was strong already.
b. the marriage was failing.
c. there were unresolved issues concerning the death of the child.

d. the parents were emotionally prepared for the event.

16. Which of these describes the current pattern of suicide rates in the United States?
a. Suicide rates decline with age.
b. The rates are higher among women than among men.
c. Men are four times as likely to succeed in committing suicide as are women.
d. Men make more attempts at suicide.

17. Deliberately withholding or discontinuing treatment that might extend the life of a terminally ill patient is called:
a. active euthanasia.
b. passive euthanasia.
c. assisted suicide.
d. advanced directive euthanasia.

18. Assisted suicide is:
a. legal in most states.
b. opposed by the American Medical Association as being contrary to the physician's oath to do no harm.
c. legal in about half of the states.
d. None of these.

19. A life review can:
a. occur at any time.
b. have special meaning in old age.
c. foster a sense of integrity.
d. All of these.

20. Dying may be a(n):
a. developmental experience.
b. unwelcome experience.
c. "good death."
d. All of these.

Short Essay Questions

These short essay questions are based on the Checkpoints in the chapter. Answer each questions as completely and succinctly as possible. Check your answers by reviewing the part of the chapter that covers the Guidepost listed with each question.

1. Give some examples of cross-cultural differences in customs and attitudes related to death. (See Guidepost 1.)

2. Briefly describe how people of different ages cope with death and bereavement. (See Table 19-2 and Guidepost 2.)

3. Discuss the ways in which an adult's loss of a spouse or parent can be a maturing experience. (See Guidepost 4.)

4. Discuss the ethical, practical, and legal issues involved in advance directives, euthanasia, and assisted suicide. (See Guidepost 4.)

Organize It!

1. List the seven illness-related concerns for patients nearing death, and the associated questions and interventions for each concern, (See Table 19-1 and Guidepost 1.)

    1.

    2.

    3.

    4.

    5.

    6.

    7.

2. List the stages of death and dying, according to Kübler-Ross's theory. (See Guidepost 2.)

    1.

    2.

    3.

    4.

    5.

3. List five common assumptions about grief and the faults associated with each assumption. (See Guidepost 2.)

    1.

    2.

    3.

    4.

    5.

3. List the three stages of grief work, according to the classic model of grief work. (See Guidepost 2.)

    1.

    2.

    3.

    4.

Critical Thinking Questions

These questions can be used for extra-credit, if your instructor agrees, or for small-group discussions.

1. If you have experienced a loss, especially an ambiguous one, how did you cope with it? What coping methods did you use?

2. What advice could you give a friend about what to say—and what not to say—to a person who is in mourning?

3. In your opinion, is the intentional ending of one's own life ever justified? Why or why not?

4. Would you ever donate an organ? To whom would you consider donating: a family member, a friend, a stranger?

5. Should assisted suicide be legalized? Why or why not?

Answer Keys

True/False Self-Test

1.	F	GP 1	11.	F	GP 3
2.	T	GP 1	12.	F	GP 3
3.	T	GP 1	13.	T	GP 4
4.	F	GP 1	14.	F	GP 4
5.	T	GP 2	15.	F	GP 4
6.	T	GP 2	16.	T	GP 4
7.	F	GP 2	17.	T	GP 4
8.	T	GP 2	18.	T	GP 5
9.	F	GP 2	19.	T	GP 5
10.	T	GP 2	20.	F	GP 5

Multiple-Choice Self-Test

1.	b	GP 1	11.	d	GP 2
2.	c	GP 1	12.	b	GP 2
3.	d	GP 1	13.	c	GP 3
4.	a	GP 1	14.	d	GP 3
5.	a	GP 2	15.	a	GP 3
6.	b	GP 2	16.	c	GP 4
7.	c	GP 2	17.	b	GP 4
8.	c	GP 2	18.	b	GP 4
9.	a	GP 2	19.	d	GP 5
10.	d	GP 2	20.	d	GP 5